MW01226514

2nd Floor – 107 East 3rd Avenue
Vancouver, BC
V5T 1C7

Go farther. Go higher. Go lean.

Strategic Lean Service

A case study of how a global IT
service delivery organization used Lean
to drive organizational transformation
and achieve customer satisfaction

Robert Oh & Sunit Prakash

STRATEGIC LEAN SERVICE: A case study of how a global IT service delivery organization used Lean to drive organizational transformation and achieve customer satisfaction is written and published by Robert Oh & Sunit Prakash.

© February 2012 Robert Oh & Sunit Prakash

Publishers: **Robert Oh,** robert@eagles-wings.info
              Sunit Prakash, sunit@sunit.co.nz
              23 Tamahine St, Maupuia, Wellington 6022, New Zealand

Editing, book and cover design:
              Chris Benge, Kapiti Print Media Ltd
              chris@kpm.co.nz

Copyright acknowledgements: all copyrights are acknowledged and
none assumed.

ISBN 978-0-473-20447-1

CONTENTS

MEET THE AUTHORS   vi

ACKNOWLEDGEMENTS   xi

FOREWORD *Ardin Vlot*   xiii

FOREWORD *Maria Koral*   xv

1 STRATEGIC LEAN *Robert Oh*   17

    In which we are introduced to the power and scope of Lean, and consider how to get the most out of it.

2 SETTING THE SCENE *Robert Oh*   23

    In which we are introduced to the organization and the challenges it faced.

3 THE CHALLENGES *Robert Oh*   29

    In which the organization's structure and predicament are spelled out in more detail.

4 THE GLOBAL SUPPORT ORGANIZATION AND CHALLENGES IN ASIA-PACIFIC-JAPAN *Sunit Prakash*   35

    In which we learn more about the global environment and focus on the contours of the APJ region.

5 A NEW CHAPTER BEGINS *Robert Oh*   43

    In which the Lean journey is envisioned and begun.

6 A NEW STRATEGY IS BORN *Robert Oh*   49

    In which we meet the organization's revolutionary new strategy and its five foundational pillars.

7 ONE, TWO, THREE . . . JUMP! *Robert Oh*   59

    In which the leadership launches its Up To Excellence transformation strategy and convinces its management to take a leap of faith.

8 FOR GOOD MEASURE: PLANNING, TRACKING AND REPORTING *Sunit Prakash* 69

    In which nothing is taken for granted any more, and comprehensive analysis and measures of performance are put in place.

9 PEOPLE POWER: HUMAN CAPITAL DEVELOPMENT *Sunit Prakash*   79

    In which the organization learns to turbo-charge its people, and makes going to work more meaningful, challenging and fun.

10 OPERATION BREEZE: PROCESS AND PERFORMANCE
IMPROVEMENT USING LEAN *Robert Oh*   89
   In which every process is critically examined, company culture
   is transformed, and success breeds success.

11 UPGRADING THE SUPPLY VALUE CHAIN:
SUPPLIER MANAGEMENT *Sunit Prakash*   101
   In which relationships with suppliers are redefined for
   the benefit of customers.

12 BEHIND THE SCENES: SUPPORT INFRASTRUCTURE,
INNOVATION AND TECHNOLOGY *Sunit Prakash*   107
   In which technology improvements under the hood make
   the ride smoother and more powerful.

13 MEASURING CUSTOMER SATISFACTION *Sunit Prakash* 113
   In which better metrics enable the organization to focus
   on making its customers happy.

14 BOULDER SHIFTING:
SMART CHANGES AND THEIR RESULTS *Sunit Prakash*   121
   In which empowered staff members run kaizens across the globe,
   with results clear for all to see.

15 NEW OPPORTUNITIES:
ADDITIONAL REVENUE, ITIL AND ISO *Sunit Prakash* 131
   In which Lean practices open doors to new business opportunities
   and quality certification.

16 ALL ABOARD: LEADERSHIP, COMMUNICATION, AND
ORGANIZATIONAL TRANSFORMATION *Robert Oh*   143
   In which a leader mines his own life experiences to communicate
   vision, and events are held to inspire, involve and leverage the
   talents of every employee.

17 REFLECTING ON OUR LEAN JOURNEY *Robert Oh*   157
   In which a leader on this journey considers its transforming
   impact – both corporate and personal – on the travellers.

18 OVER TO YOU *Robert Oh*   171
   In which the authors wish you success as you progress
   on your own Lean journey.

GLOSSARY   175

▶ ▶ ▶ ▶ ▶ ▶ ▶ ▶ ▶ ▶ ▶ ▶ ▶ ▶ ▶ ▶

This book is dedicated to technical product support analysts and engineers around the world, and to all those who assist them to deliver top class service to their customers.

▶ ▶ ▶ ▶ ▶ ▶ ▶ ▶ ▶ ▶ ▶ ▶ ▶ ▶ ▶ ▶

MEET THE AUTHORS

ROBERT OH was Vice-President of Baan Customer Service & Support, Asia Pacific Japan (APJ), charged with running Baan CS&S's strategic improvement project (codenamed Breeze) on a global basis, utilizing Lean as the platform to drive change.

SUNIT PRAKASH was Director Operations, Baan Customer Service & Support APJ, responsible for operationally realising the benefits of Lean in the APJ region.

ROBERT OH AND SUNIT PRAKASH have collaborated in this book to bring you their remarkable shared experience of deploying strategic Lean Service at Baan CS&S in the first years of the new millennium under the leadership of Ardin Vlot (then Senior Vice-President of the global support organization). To do this they have each contributed a number of chapters to this story. Authorship of each chapter is identified at the chapter's outset.

This book is a story, not a textbook. The authors do not offer you checklist upon checklist to tick off what you have and have not done in your deployment of Lean in comparison to the Baan CS&S experience. However, a short summary of learning points – called *Lean Pickings* – has been provided at the end of each chapter.

▶ ROBERT OH

MBA, BEEng, British Computer Society Exams (Part 1 & 2), Senior Member of Singapore Computer Society, Member of IT Management Association

Robert Oh is the founder and principal of *Eagles Wings*, a Lean Six Sigma consulting and training firm based in Singapore. He is an experienced leader in the areas of operations, product development and project management, with more than twenty years of IT experience. His wide-ranging experience includes global and regional leadership positions in industry.

Beginning his career at the Singapore National Computer Board, Robert was deployed at Ministry of Home Affairs working on applications development. He subsequently moved on to lead the data centre and technical teams there.

In 1987 Robert led a task force to study opportunities for nationwide implementation of Electronic Data Interchange (EDI). This led to his joining Singapore Network Services (SNS), which built and operated the world's first EDI trade documentation clearance system involving all air, land and sea links. This world-renowned system aggressively targeted the reduction of paperwork and waste associated with import and export documentation and clearance. At SNS he managed the technical support and networking teams, the customer service centre and data centre operations. He joined Baan in 1997.

Over the last decade Robert has been closely involved in providing clients with Lean and Lean Six Sigma consulting and education services to help them improve their processes and organizational performance. His engagements have brought him to the US, Europe and Asia Pacific. His Lean process improvement experience spans areas as diverse as customer service to software development, air travel catering services to supply chain logistics, and manufacturing to maintenance repair and overhaul services.

As a Thought Leader on the subject of Lean, Robert speaks at conferences and contributes his ideas, views and concerns to business and technical publications. He is a consultant, educator and researcher of Lean and Lean Six Sigma.

Robert is passionate about Lean. He longs to see enlightened organizations keep ahead of the growing competition around them by leveraging Lean to its fullest potential.

When he is not working, Robert focuses on family time and helps church communities by teaching and providing personal counselling on emotional healing.

For more information visit: http://www.eagles-wings.info/
Robert can be contacted via email: robert@eagles-wings.info

► SUNIT PRAKASH

MBA, BSc, Member New Zealand Computer Society, IT Certified Professional, Certified ISO 20000 Consultant

Sunit Prakash gravitated into the business of customer satisfaction and technical product support in 1987 when he was selected as an AIESEC trainee administering third-level support to the field for IBM in Sweden.

Now based in New Zealand, Sunit has worked in management and consulting roles with global and specialist niche ICT organizations across a number of sectors including Banking & Finance, Power Utilities, Telcos, Health, Local Government and Gaming.

His work has focused on assisting them in all aspects of their service management initiatives – defining ICT models, architecting IT service management models, outlining frameworks and requirements, reviewing supplier contracts and performance, contract negotiations and procurement, project managing transition to, and the implementation of, new models – to improve customer satisfaction by better, more effective provision of IT services to end users.

During his career he has managed, optimized or transitioned more than twenty Service Desks covering hardware from desktops and servers through to ATMs, voice & data networks, customer relationship management software, financial accounting packages, warehouse management systems, supply chain management solutions, and enterprise resource planning systems.

Sunit has been active at a local and national level in IT Service Management Forum (itSMF) in New Zealand. He instigated the Service Management Project of the Year Award and was the convenor of the judging panel.

He has reviewed international service management publications, presented at conferences, run workshops and training sessions and been in the national press on Lean Transformation, IT Service Management, Business & Technology in India, and the use of Social Media for Small & Medium Businesses.

When Sunit is not improving customer satisfaction, he is out four-wheel driving, or airing his classic Royal Enfield Bullet motorcycle.

You can follow Sunit on Twitter: @sunitprakash
For more information visit: http://www.sunit.co.nz
Sunit can be contacted via email: sunit@sunit.co.nz

ACKNOWLEDGEMENTS

WE WOULD LIKE TO THANK ARDIN Vlot and Maria Koral, without whom there would have been no Lean journey for us to undertake, and this book would not have been possible.

We would also like to thank Herman Steijger. Together Ardin, Maria and Herman reviewed our manuscript, provided suggestions and inputs, and were always encouraging of our endeavour.

We contacted as many members of the Baan Customer Service and Support Team as we could for their stories, views and vignettes amplifying and confirming what we wrote. For we wanted to show that this was not just *our* story or journey; that it was not just how *we* felt; that it was not just *our* lives on which this transformation had such a profound impact. And so our sincere thanks to Sonja de Feijter, Gert den Hertog, Heymen Jansen, Osama Kort, Mathew Loxton, Santosh Menon, Ravi Kabbur, Jordi Morillas, Noel Sebastian, Shinya Takahashi, Rajeev Dixit and Stefan Verbeek – for their contributions, and for validating from every corner of the globe our thoughts, feelings and discoveries.

We also thought it important to get input from someone removed from and impartial to our journey – thanks to John Seah for reviewing the early manuscript and providing feedback.

Of course, our thanks and acknowledgements would not be complete if we did not recognize the hard work put in very patiently by Chris Benge our editor, who struggled sometimes with the passion of our arcane journey!

FOREWORD BY ARDIN VLOT

THE TRUE IMPACT OF A TRANSFORMATION program can be fully appreciated only after the event.

At the start you can use your imagination to picture a successful outcome, plan for it by setting direction and objectives, agree on the approaches and tactics to be followed, and negotiate required resources. But despite it all you remain unsure. Will it work or not?

When we started our turnaround project to drastically improve the customer service division in Baan/Invensys, this is how we felt. With only limited experience in the fields of customer service and Lean transformation, we felt inadequate and apprehensive when we looked at the task ahead.

Our situation was spelled out frankly. My boss at the time, Laurens van der Tang, made it quietly clear: "We are in turmoil because of missed quarters, management 'jumping ship', and other misery. Our strategy moving forward can only be to focus on selling new and existing product to our customer base. That will only happen if this customer base is extremely happy. Go fix it!"

What followed was a fascinating roller coaster ride with a group of people who clearly achieved more than they had ever imagined they could. I think this book gives you a sense of that. Honestly, that is what I felt was the greatest reward of all: helping people perform much better than they believed they could by encouraging them to 'step out of their own circle'.

And the customers? They loved it. They could see the improvement, they could sense the culture change, and they appreciated the improved performance. Every day we monitored their response, and our teams were further encouraged by it.

I hope the reader of this book, interested in the practicalities of managing change, will enjoy this ride as much as we did.

Because time goes by fast, and many of our fellows have meanwhile explored other opportunities, please allow me to say one more thing to the 600-odd employees who were part of this journey: Thank you guys. Great job!

Ardin M.C. Vlot
Chief Inspiration Officer at Exalio Group BV,
Barneveld, The Netherlands
ardinmcvlot@exalio.com

FOREWORD BY MARIA KORAL

WHEN I FIRST MET ARDIN VLOT, Senior VP Customer Service and Support, he mentioned that he had some knowledge and experience with Lean methods and principles. After learning about my role as a Lean Transformation Consultant, he asked if I would be interested in working with him and his team to drive improvement initiatives in his organization. My first reaction was to say no. After all, my experience had been mainly in manufacturing environments and not in Software Customer Service and Support. After a brief discussion, we agreed to give it a try but with an understanding that it may not work.

The first challenge was to take my manufacturing-based training materials and, without changing the principles, translate it to more software engineering-friendly language. Working with a small group from Ardin's team made this process a breeze.

After identifying the key business challenges, such as backlog of cases, resolution time and the need for performance measurement systems, we started mapping processes, changing systems and business practices at a steady and continuous pace. Results were seen almost immediately. Most impressive to me was that results were shown on all three continents – a clear sign that vision, strategy and objectives were well defined and communicated throughout the organization.

The Baan team is still in my heart today. It was a pleasure to work with a talented group that was eager to learn, open to changes and excited about the results. There was never a shortage of fantastic celebrations of accomplishments. Without a doubt, this was one of the most rewarding and fun projects of my career.

Maria Koral
Business Transformation Consultant
(Lean Sensei from Invensys at the time of Operation Breeze)
koral@attglobal.net

1

STRATEGIC LEAN

Robert Oh

In which we are introduced to the power and scope of Lean, and consider how to get the most out of it.

AS COMPETITION INCREASES ACROSS THE WORLD in every market in industry, companies are continually searching for ways to become better and more competitive. They are striving to gain that extra edge, to expand their capabilities, to increase productivity and efficiency, and to deploy whatever scarce resources they have in more optimal ways so that they can beat the competition in whatever they do.

In searching for new, better ways of doing things, many companies have adopted Lean to provide more value, deliver their goods or services more quickly, and turn in higher profits by reducing their costs. Lean, originally developed by Toyota to build better quality cars with shorter turnaround times and at lower costs than their competitors, has been the main reason why Toyota became the world's most successful and profitable auto-manufacturer.

Lean is not just deployed in Toyota's plants. It is used in their marketing approach, their product development centres, and their supply chain and distribution networks. It is used by their parts distribution centres, their sales distributors, and is

Lean is used in every part of Toyota

deployed at their vehicle repair workshops and those of their distributors. It is used to schedule and to carry out routine vehicle maintenance for customers... and the list goes on and on. Lean is used in absolutely every part of Toyota.

Over the last two decades Lean's concepts and principles were adopted by countless other manufacturing companies who embraced the same ideas about cutting waste and making continuous ongoing improvement. As Lean came to be accepted more and more widely throughout the manufacturing space, it also jumped over to service industries. Hospitals and other healthcare agencies, maintenance repair and overhaul companies for cars, buses and aircraft, food catering firms, banks, insurance companies, government agencies, the military, the oil and gas industry, educational institutions and so many others have now embraced and deployed Lean.

Having worked with many different firms from many industries, and on hundreds of kaizen projects (or 'rapid improvement' projects, as they are sometimes called), I realize that Lean contains much potential that is still untapped by many of its users. Too many companies have adopted Lean only at the operational level. Even many of those firms that appear to deploy Lean strategically have failed to do so in the correct way.

There are already many books written about Lean. These publications cover topics ranging from the need to build the appropriate organizational culture so that a continuous improvement journey, once begun, can be sustained in the long term, to a full set of Lean tools and techniques – the 'hardware' of Lean. Taking steps to form the right organizational culture, and training personnel to understand and use Lean's simple but powerful tools and techniques, are both very important. But these are piecemeal measures taken in an attempt to ramp up Lean skills and sustain the Lean journey. They are not sufficient in themselves to ensure the journey is sustainable long term.

What is needed is an appropriate strategic approach to deploying Lean: a strategic approach in which all elements or pillars of an organization's strategy fully embrace Lean, and where there are no gaps in the strategy vis-à-vis Lean; where there are no gaps in the deployment of Lean; where initiatives and tactics in every part of the organization will support, not contradict Lean, nor create un-Lean behaviour.

This is the reason this book has been written. So many companies are attempting to deploy Lean without fully building Lean into their strategies. Plants are being told to become leaner, produce with shorter lead times, cut inventory – but the global supply planning department still continues to order parts based on forecast, not on what the customer is buying. Bosses are trying to promote teamwork, but they are making no headway because their employee compensation systems are currently designed to motivate individual performance rather than team performance. Leaders are emphasizing the need to skill up for Lean, but the training department doesn't understand that upskilling on Lean tools and techniques is not all that is needed.

Lean has brought about an awareness of new and important measurements like Lead Time and First Time Right Rate, but the organization is still not able to measure them in a reliable way across its offices. Kaizens are being executed in many parts of the organization, management is speaking about them, but employees are not able to see how these efforts relate to their own or the company's goals. Lean has been deployed for several years in a firm, but the approval process for purchases is still long and unwieldy. Queues at service counters are getting shorter and shorter because of quicker processing times and higher First Time Right processing, but the month-end closing of the accounts still takes these firms two weeks every month to complete. The organization has been doing Lean for several years, but every year the ISO audits still take up an inordinate amount of time and effort.

This book has been written to illustrate how companies ought to deploy Lean – that is, how to deploy Lean in a *fully strategic* manner. Thus far little has been published about strategic Lean deployment, particularly where that involves real-life experiences or the case studies of real companies. *Deploying Strategic Lean,* as we have chosen to call this approach, requires embracing Lean in every part or pillar of your strategy. If done correctly, it will create a very powerful force to drive long term change and improvement.

This book uses as a case study the Lean journey undertaken by the Baan Customer Service and Support (CS&S) organization – probably the first worldwide implementation of Lean in such a services context. While its context or industry may differ from yours, the basic principles and approach for deploying Lean in such a strategic manner remain widely applicable.

Central to our view of Lean deployment is that it is not only essential *what* steps you take, but also *how well* you do each of them. For example, not only is it important that you communicate your organization's vision, strategy and goals to your employees: it is even more important *how well* you manage to communicate this to them. Let's pick another example: marketing, for instance. Every company does marketing, but few are as successful as Toyota at finding out what customers want in their automobiles. So doing it is one thing; how well you are able to do it is another. Readers ought to keep this in mind as they read this book.

We have tried to include in this story all the key stages of our journey to help readers understand these events, beginning from the incubation stages right through to successful accomplish-

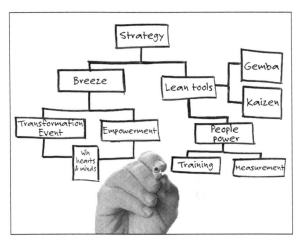

We cover all key stages of the CS&S Lean journey

ment of Baan CS&S's initial goals. We cover how the journey began for Baan CS&S; how issues and feedback from customers – both internal and external – were gathered and used; and how the Up To Excellence strategy was developed, the thinking behind it, and all the pillars of this fully Lean-embracing strategy.

We include an account of how the organization-wide performance improvement drive, Operation Breeze, was kicked off and sustained for the long term, and how employees were engaged to run together in the same direction towards the same goals. And we tell of how these aggressive goals were ultimately achieved.

While Baan CS&S's Lean journey lasted four years beginning in 2000 and ending in 2004, it would have very likely continued for the long term had Baan not been sold by Invensys to SSA Global Technologies during the tough recession years of 2002–2003. However, in spite of this journey being only four years long, we believe its telling offers many valuable insights. It was an amazing journey for those of us fortunate enough to be a part of it.

May you enjoy journeying with us as we share this previously untold story with you – and may you find it valuable in assisting you as your organization continues its own journey into Lean transformation.

2

SETTING THE SCENE
Robert Oh

*In which we are introduced to the organization
and the challenges it faced.*

IT WAS AUTUMN OF THE YEAR 2000. The great Y2K stampede to buy, install and cut over to new software was over. Enterprises all around the world were no longer spending a lot of money. Revenues for software licenses had fallen; likewise, spending on IT services had dwindled.

In this new era after Y2K, software companies shifted their spotlights to an area they had hitherto taken for granted: their support and maintenance revenue streams. New product development for software was largely going to depend on these revenue streams. They were vitally important to ensure customer loyalty for the long term.

Baan, however, faced even bigger challenges. Once the second largest software company in Europe, Baan had been acquired by Invensys a few months earlier. Laurens van der Tang, a long time Baan stalwart appointed as its new CEO, had carefully taken the company through a rigorous but rapid restructuring and cost management program. Now this was all completed, a new set of challenges awaited.

The book Lean Transformation *by Henderson & Larco which Ardin Vlot found so helpful*

Customers had concerns about Baan's future. Would Baan survive? Would the promised software enhancements be delivered? These fears had to be alleviated quickly. Additionally, many customers were unhappy with the level of support they were receiving from CS&S. They felt resolutions to their calls were taking way too long; bug-fixes didn't always bring the expected results. Customers were saying that CS&S was not proactive enough in how it engaged with customers. Customer reference ability had fallen significantly – to a historic low.

Upon his new appointment as Senior Vice-President of CS&S, the first task for Ardin Vlot (formerly Vice-President of Development, and before that Managing Director Baan Netherlands) was the development of a new strategy to restore customer confidence and raise the CS&S Division to new heights. Vlot had recently received a book entitled *Lean Transformation,* and he spent much time mulling it over as he thought about the new CS&S strategy he had started to plan.

What should be done to drive improvement across the globe? How could CS&S drastically cut the existing call backlog? What area should it attack first? How could it build an effective and full-fledged strategy covering all the key knobs that needed to be turned? The book, written by Invensys senior executive Bruce Henderson (who headed the newly created Invensys Software Systems of which Baan was now a part), together with Jorge Larco, had thrown up a myriad of new ideas.

Lean

The concept of Lean originated in the mid-1990s when MIT researchers, eager to discover why Japanese automakers were so successful compared to Americans, studied Toyota and other Japanese auto-producers and coined the term 'Lean' to describe what they found. 'Lean' is not an acronym. The term was adopted because it evokes images of speed, flexibility, agility and streamlining. It is often combined with the word 'transformation' to describe the major changes to organization culture, management style, systems, processes, people and skills that take place in an organization which embraces Lean fully.

Even though the book had been written for manufacturing companies, many of the Lean concepts and principles seemed applicable to the CS&S Division. Waste was everywhere in companies, and surely CS&S had its fair share. Teamwork needed to be improved across the customer support centres. Morale was low after the acquisition, although it was slowly improving. Units tended to operate within their own silos. Customer escalations were far too commonplace, and re-sources were severely strained. Furthermore, the quality of solutions provided to customers was not always satisfactory.

Even as new Lean-inspired conceptions took shape in his head, Vlot was aware that Lean had never been used outside the manufacturing space for such a large scale and strategic ef-fort – certainly not in any industries even remotely similar to this one. CS&S would be heading into uncharted waters.

The first step any organization needs to take towards improve-ment is to recognize and acknowledge that there are problems. Once this is done, and managers and employees can speak openly about the issues they face, a door has been opened for improvements to follow. There was no doubt that there were issues in CS&S, and that things needed to change and be improved – and quickly.

LEAN PICKINGS

► Lateral thinking is required for problem solving. It is sometimes possible to apply manufacturing-related solutions to services.

► The organization should recognise and acknowledge that there are problems that need to be resolved.

► Take a customer view.

► Create an environment which supports management and staff speaking openly about the issues.

3

THE CHALLENGES
Robert Oh

In which the organization's structure and
predicament are spelled out in more detail.

CS&S's WORLDWIDE ORGANIZATION COMPRISED MORE than
twenty support centres around the globe, supported by three
large Product Engineering Group (PEG) centres located
in the Netherlands, the US and India. Reporting to Ardin
Vlot were the Vice-Presidents of the three regions: Sonja
de Feijter for Europe, Middle East and Africa (EMEA), Ken
Crossman for the Americas, and Robert Oh for Asia-Pacific-
Japan (APJ). EMEA had the largest customer base, followed
by the Americas. Herman Steijger was the Business Controller
CS&S, and Gert den Hertog was Vice-President PEG.

Every region was experiencing a large backlog of reported
cases; this was paralleled by the backlog of software defects
at PEG centres. As a company we had grown rapidly and now
had a large customer base, and customer support needs had
grown in tandem over the previous few years. Despite rapidly expanding our support capabilities and engaging support
partners to pick up some of the workload, the backlog of cases
had built to unprecedented levels. With the restructuring that
followed the Invensys acquisition, this backlog now looked
more formidable than ever.

CS&S sought customer feedback through quarterly surveys

There was no doubt at this point that customer confidence had taken a big hit, and customer satisfaction was near its lowest-ever levels. For some time we had already been doing quarterly customer surveys to gauge customer sentiment. The worldwide overall Customer Satisfaction Gap score for the latest quarterly customer survey was at a whopping 3.4 level (the Gap score measured the difference between customers' expectations of service levels, and what they perceived CS&S was delivering to them).

The Gap score of 4.0 for Time to Provide Solution was even more severe, reflecting the long resolution times customers experienced waiting for solutions. Quality of Solution was only slightly better at 3.5. Customer Reference Ability concerning support and maintenance services was at a low of 60%. (Sunit Prakash goes into more detail about metrics in Chapter 8.)

The case backlog had now reached an unprecedented worldwide level of 10,000. These were not trivial cases requiring only a couple of minutes to resolve. Most of them were technical difficulties customers were facing, as well as software defects that needed to be fixed.

Based on customer feedback, the situation was rather bleak. Baan CS&S was in a vulnerable position. Customer complaint handling and case escalation was consuming an inordinate amount of time – and in some cases the complaints were about to become lawsuits. We urgently needed to bring down the huge backlog of cases in order to reduce our resolution time and improve customer satisfaction.

Metric	Position
Overall Satisfaction	3.4 Gap Score
Time to Provide Solution	4.0 Gap Score
Quality of Solution	3.5 Gap score
Customer Reference Ability	60%
Backlog of Reported Cases	10,000 cases

The bleak situation in which CS&S found itself

There was a clear need to regain the initiative and move into a more proactive mode. We needed to work with Baan Development to ensure that software testing was intensified, so that all new software released would be of better quality than it had been before. This would reduce the number of incoming calls to CS&S support centres.

Software bug-fixes and patches had to be delivered more quickly once defects were discovered in the field, so that other customers would not experience the same problems and add to the calls coming in. We also needed to develop and roll out software tools to consider and check automatically for pre-requisite patches in order to help customers install bug-fixes correctly. This would make it easier for customers to install these patches and, once again, reduce unnecessary calls. Better systems and knowledge bases were needed so that customers could more easily access solutions over the internet and install these themselves.

Worldwide our processes and services varied significantly, requiring standardization and streamlining. We urgently needed systems to facilitate collaboration across the globe, so that teams didn't have to reinvent the wheel when faced with 'known' problems – especially issues that had already been reported and solved elsewhere. Skill sets needed to be ramped up. There was insufficient cross-skilling taking place.

While some level of cooperation existed across the various support centres and PEGs, there was great potential for deepening that cooperation across the organization. This was paralleled by other opportunities for increased cooperation with the rest of Baan, in particular Sales and Consulting, as well as with Baan Development, the Research & Development arm of Baan.

In the next chapter my colleague Sunit Prakash explains more about how Baan CS&S was organized, and its role in Baan. He describes the overall Baan organization structure within which CS&S operated, and the organizational tensions that existed as a result – tensions common to so many other companies in this industry.

LEAN PICKINGS

► Obtain feedback about what customers think about your products and services on a regular basis. This is so that trends can be spotted. Ensure that the feedback information is specific enough to be acted on.

► The Gap score is an effective measure of the difference between customers' expectations of service levels and what customers perceive the organization is actually delivering to them.

► The long waiting time before customers received solutions to their cases was due to the amount of time the cases spent in queues and waiting.

► Taking action to reduce the number of calls coming in (eg. providing more self-help options) was as important as taking action to work on and clear the large backlog of cases.

4

THE GLOBAL SUPPORT ORGANIZATION AND CHALLENGES IN ASIA-PACIFIC-JAPAN

Sunit Prakash

In which we learn more about the global environment and focus on the contours of the APJ region.

BAAN WAS A NASDAQ-LISTED ENTERPRISE RESOURCE Planning (ERP) vendor. Founded by Jan & Paul Baan in the Netherlands, it counted Boeing amongst its largest customers. The ERP space at that time was known as BOPS – Baan, Oracle, PeopleSoft and SAP. Gartner put Baan in the 'visionary' quadrant.

Each of Baan's three global regions was headed by a Regional President, to whom individual Country Managers reported. The Country Managers in turn ran the local sales teams and carried responsibility, primarily for the numbers of software license sales. This sales structure was mirrored in the consulting arm, and also within CS&S.

While the local consulting arm was responsible for implementation of the new license sales (often complemented by partners), CS&S was responsible for post-implementation technical product support. Customers paid revenues in the form of

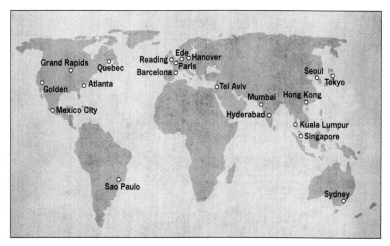

Baan Customer Service and Support centres across the world

support and maintenance on an annual basis, and these were often calculated as a percentage of license fees. The purchase of support and maintenance entitled customers to help desk support for technical issues, and also – importantly – to new versions and releases of the software. With a growing installed base, support and maintenance fees were the revenue engine feeding the sales force and the development teams. Industry analysts would keep a close eye on both license revenues and support and maintenance revenues to tell if a company was growing or stagnant.

As the enterprise market grew more saturated after Y2K and new customers became harder to find, larger players in the ERP market started moving down into the SME (small and medium enterprise) space. More importantly, some started acquiring market share by buying software companies with large installed customer bases. The recurring support and maintenance revenues attracted them, and their acquisitions of smaller players (or ERP vendors) often protected customers' initial license investments by offering them a technology upgrade path.

Underpinned by a single global case management system and other related infrastructure, CS&S was different from Sales and Consulting in that it had built relatively consistent, global systems and processes. It was therefore able to operate effectively as a global organization, rather than simply as a cluster of local organizations held together within regional organizations. At times tensions arose at local country level, where the Country Manager was responsible not only for carrying the license numbers, but also for the country operations. Generally Consulting reported to the Country Managers, but CS&S centres within the country had a matrix reporting structure, reporting both to the local Country Manager and also to the Regional Support Vice-President.

Local sales people, primarily incentivized for new license sales, sometimes discounted support and maintenance to close the license deal. This did nothing to help in-country tensions! Add to this an aggressive product release policy, a growing stable of products covering now not only ERP but also Customer Relationship Management (CRM) and Supply Chain Management (SCM), quality issues that arose in the field, and the need to support these products on a plethora of hardware platforms, operating systems and databases, and life and challenges for CS&S were always interesting. . . .

The APJ region faced additional challenges. Products not only had to be localized for many of the countries in the region, but for China, Japan and Korea they also had to be multibyte enabled and translated – and the second-level support centre was quite a distance away in India, and for them in another language. Furthermore, if solution development had to be done, it could be worked on in either India, Europe or the US – making communication even more challenging because of further time zone differences!

All these meant that complexities in the APJ region were higher than in other regions of the world! Localization differences, language differences, time zone differences, multibyte differences . . . the APJ CS&S operation had to face and overcome all these various challenges.

To keep the CS&S organization in APJ close to customers and to ensure maximum responsiveness to them, the region was organized with local support centres in all the major sub-regions of Japan, Korea, China, ASEAN (located in Malaysia and Singapore), India and Australia. This was done to increase customer confidence in support and language capability in terms of reach and nearness to customers, enabling rapid deployment to customer sites to handle critical situations, and also increasing understanding and familiarity with the localizations made to the software. Placing support centres in each sub-region also allowed them to coordinate more closely with any sales efforts underway, which meant (for example) giving special attention to large prospects. Communications between the local support and consulting teams also improved

Cross-Cultural Collaboration

What I remember best about this challenging and encouraging period was the international cooperation within PEG and the whole of CS&S. Different cultures have sometimes quite different approaches and perspectives. In a team it is useful to have that kind of variety.

As a strong team we were able to utilize each other's strengths and competencies. In some areas Americans were best, in others our Indian colleagues, and in some others the Dutch guys. This also is the challenge for a service organization that delivers to customers around the world. Customers

dramatically, enabling better coordination and efforts to support those customers undergoing implementation.

This approach ran counter to the conventional wisdom of the day, which insisted on centralizing resources to achieve the benefits arising from critical mass. In fact these support centres achieved such benefits using an alternate and clever approach: joining ranks with local consulting teams and sharing infrastructure with them created sufficient critical mass. This also resulted in strengthened cooperation between support centres and local consulting teams.

Even though this approach seemed to increase the challenges of running the CS&S APJ operation, Robert Oh had decided early on that this was the best way for us to organize ourselves to support customers in this region. We were to look and make decisions from the perspective of the customer and not from the perspective of how difficult it would be to run the operation, a key principle of Lean – to adopt an outside-looking-

have their own culture and behaviour which may be best understood by teams in the same country or region. Here we found we could help each other out to become even more international, or should I say 'intercultural'.

The CS&S journey itself also changed the culture in our teams and in the entire organization. I strongly believe that the leadership of Ardin and the rest of the management team was crucial in getting things to move in the right direction at the desired speed. I remember we referenced the change model by John Kotter, starting with a strong sense of urgency.

Bottom line: we deal with people. And what can be more challenging and rewarding than that? Understanding people and working with them is the challenge for all managers, no matter what country, no matter what organization, no matter what culture.

Gert den Hertog
Vice-President PEG

into-the-company perspective rather than an inside-looking-out perspective. We were not to prioritize to make it easy to run our own operations, but instead prioritize what was best for the customers – and then find a way to make our operations work to deliver those priorities.

In the next chapter our Lean journey begins. It began by taking steps to find out what customers thought of us and what they really wanted. Following this, feedback was solicited from employees by 'going to the ground' and speaking with them to find out what issues they were facing, and to seek their opinion on what needed to be done.

LEAN PICKINGS

▶ The value proposition for support and maintenance is 1) easy and quick access to technical support for software issues, and 2) the protection afforded by an upward migration path of the software.

▶ Despite language and software differences, to be effective worldwide it is important to set up and operate a support and maintenance organization with globally standard infrastructure and processes.

▶ The complexity due to language, localization, multibyte and time zone differences is the greatest in the APJ region and this creates additional challenges which do not exist in the other regions.

▶ The placement of support centres in each sub-region of APJ meant that support analysts could reach customers to assist them in the shortest possible time in the event of any critical failure to their system. This is fundamentally Lean in approach.

▶ When making strategic decisions, the perspective of the customer often takes precedence over the ease of running your own operations, as seen in the organizational structure adopted by the CS&S APJ region.

5

A NEW CHAPTER BEGINS
Robert Oh

In which the Lean journey is envisioned and begun.

ARDIN VLOT KNEW HE HAD TO move quickly to establish a firm footing upon which to drive change. Much had to be done.

The first order of things was to find out more about Lean transformation. Till that time in 2000, Lean had been used primarily by manufacturing companies. No-one had ever contemplated any large-scale global implementation of Lean beyond the manufacturing sector. CS&S was certainly not a manufacturing company. It was an intriguing possibility: to use Lean concepts and principles in a way and on a scale that had never been done before.

The next step was to solicit input both from customers and from employees within the organization, to understand more precisely what the issues were. Even though several years of surveys had already amassed quite a lot of information about what our customers wanted from us, it was necessary to hear directly from them what they saw as value, what they were willing to pay for, and what was important to them, rather than try to make educated guesses.

Definition of *Value*

Value is defined as what 'the customer is willing to pay for'. *Value-added* activities are the activities that employees in organizations perform, for which their customers are willing to pay. Conversely, *non-value-added* activities are those activities that are performed for which the customers are not willing to pay. Non-value-added activities which are not required are considered waste.

So Vlot began a round-the-world trip to 'go to gemba', meeting with both customers and employees to learn what their concerns were, and to hear their thoughts and suggestions for improvement. At the same time he sought and obtained the help of Maria Koral, a Lean Sensei from Invensys.

The meetings with employees were called Tea Sessions. These sessions were informal, without any kind of fixed format. Vlot just chatted with the employees over tea and cakes to find out what the problems, issues and wastes were in the organiza-

Go To Gemba

Gemba means 'actual' or 'real place' in Japanese. Going to the actual place or going to the 'ground' to see what really happens is one of the key principles of Lean. True Lean managers rely heavily on firsthand observation, ie. direct observation, to learn what customers feel, what they are saying and whether their needs are being met. This is an effective way to know how well an organization actually performs in serving its customers. Lean managers also frequently go to gemba within their own organizations to discover what the organization's problems are, and what truly happens in their organizations.

tion. What problems did customers face? What difficulties did employees have? What suggestions or remedies could they propose? Eight key threads began to emerge from his discussions with them.

Going to gemba is the start of fixing the problems

The Eight Key Issues

1. **We do not keep our promises to our customers** – we often miss the solution deadlines (called the Promised Solution Date) that we promise to customers. This upsets the customers, particularly when they have had to wait for quite a long time already for the promised solution.

2. **Our solutions knowledge base needs to be cleaned up** – multiple 'solutions' to the same problem are often found in the knowledge base, but customers and employees often don't know the appropriate one to use. Some of the solutions are outdated, and others contain errors. These solutions are created and documented by different individuals from various CS&S centres around the world, and there is no standard way to do this, nor is there any kind of quality check before they are made available to customers and internal employees.

3. **Lack of a proper patch installation tool** – there is no proper tool to help customers install their software patches, so they often make errors in the process. To make matters worse, the customizations made by customers to the source code are not reflected in standard patches that are developed and released by the PEG centres to fix defects in the software, and customers are not

always aware of this or the implications of this when they install patches.

4. **We do not update customers on the status of their cases** – customers do not receive updates from the support centres after they log their case. After the call is placed, the support centre does not keep the customer updated on the progress of the work.

5. **Customers are not using the solutions knowledge base** – not enough customers are using the knowledge base to find solutions for themselves. Instead of using the knowledge base available over the internet as a self-help facility, customers tend to log a case with the CS&S support centres.

6. **Our response time for new cases is too long** – customers say that we take too long before responding to them, and in some cases don't tell them that we are starting work on their case.

7. **The quality of our solutions is not good enough** – quite often solutions provided to customers have to be reworked. Too many of the bug-fixes and workarounds provided to customers have errors in them, or are defective. The quality of our solutions needs to be improved.

8. **Localization software quality is lacking** – in many countries a part of the software is adapted to meet local conditions and legal requirements. In many cases the poor quality of the localized software causes additional problems for customers. On top of that, the software patches developed by PEG are suitable only on the standard software, and these patches also have to be adapted for the localized software.

This list of eight issues formed the main operational boulders in CS&S's path. Evidently there was much work to be done. The starting point for making improvements in any organization is to be able to identify and recognize what problems and issues you face. Armed with this information, you can then make efforts to overcome them. We knew what was wrong, and that we had to fix the issues – and quickly.

Elements of a new game plan started to be put into place

Having gained a good appreciation of the current situation, Vlot now had to focus on putting together the strategy for CS&S to go forward. This new strategy needed not just to *consider* Lean, but to embrace it fully *in every part*.

So we went for it! For us it was the beginning of a new chapter, the launch into a new journey. Over the next 18 to 24 months our new strategy was deployed, and each of these issues was actively worked on and resolved, substantially or fully, across the CS&S organization worldwide. This new strategy is described in the next chapter.

LEAN PICKINGS

▶ A critical initial step in defining a new organizational strategy is to gather information and feedback to identify the problems, issues and wastes that the organization is facing. This needs to be done from three perspectives: the perspective of customers, and the perspectives of both managers and employees of the organization.

▶ This three-way input provides the leader with a complete perspective.

▶ This is done by spending time on the ground. Do not rely on data – go and see for yourself!

▶ Going to the ground demonstrates to both customers and employees the leader's interest in and commitment to making improvements.

6

A NEW STRATEGY IS BORN

Robert Oh

In which we meet the organization's revolutionary new strategy and its five foundational pillars.

EVEN AS ARDIN VLOT BEGAN HIS visits to customers and CS&S sites, he started to form a new vision and strategy. The vision was clear: to become Best In Class for customer support.

This new vision and strategy had to address all our customers' key concerns in terms that could be easily understood by both customers and employees. They also had to be tangible and measurable, simple to grasp, and capable of being translated into clear targets.

Business goals employees could relate to were needed quickly for this new vision and strategy. Vlot knew that the 'go forward journey' begins once you firmly establish the business goals – and that these goals had to be aggressive. These were crafted to cover several key customer satisfaction and operational targets:

Metric	Goal
Overall Customer Satisfaction Gap	<2.0
Gap Score Average	<1.0
Response Time	<2 hours
Resolution Time	<5 days
Quality of Solutions	>99%
Predictability of Solutions	>99%

Goals of the new strategy

The Overall Customer Satisfaction Gap was a comprehensive measure of customer happiness taken from the regular customer satisfaction surveys CS&S was already running. These surveys provided a vital source of feedback about customer needs and satisfaction levels. The feedback had to be actionable, and was used to guide management in determining areas to focus on internally in order to satisfy customers.

The Gap Score Average was an average of the measurement results for all the various areas of service in the customer survey. The gap identified the difference between how customers rated the importance of an area of service, and how well they perceived CS&S to be delivering it. The smaller the gap the better.

One obvious area of interest for many customers was Response Time. This was defined as the period from the time when the call was first placed by the customer, to the time when a call was made back to the customer by the support centre. This was also the time when actual work began on the customer's issue.

The fourth goal, Resolution Time, measured the time from which the customer placed the call to the time the case was resolved and finally closed. Because of its large backlog of cases this was CS&S's greatest challenge.. Many cases queued for long periods of time before they were eventually worked on and resolved, and so their resolution time was substantially extended. Pressure from customers for action to resolve this issue was rising, and there was no time to waste!

The source of the problem was the huge backlog of cases in the queue, which at this time numbered around 10,000. Cut the backlog and the queue time of cases could be reduced significantly. But the backlog had been growing for years, and every single initiative to reduce this backlog had never succeeded: special programs, temporary help from partners, assistance from the consulting organization, deployment of R&D personnel. Even outsourcing arrangements over the previous couple of years to take on the load of the cases from small and medium-sized customers had met with only limited success. The large backlog of cases remained and grew.

The quality of our solutions was another area of frequent complaint. Customers were saying that a fair percentage of solutions to their questions, workarounds, bug-fixes and patches were incorrect or didn't always work. In some cases client customizations turned out to be the cause of the problem, or customers had wrongly applied the solution to their system; but clearly in other cases our solutions were faulty. We needed to improve this situation immediately.

The last area of major concern was reliably predicting when a solution would become available. When we promised a solution and gave the customer a date when it would be ready, we had to be able to meet that promised date in most cases. Currently we were not able to achieve our promised solution dates for a sizeable percentage of cases due to the large backlog of calls we faced. At other times we didn't give a promised resolution date at all, because our people felt they really didn't know when the solution would be ready for the customer!

We clearly needed a bold strategy to solve all these issues and help us achieve our goals . . . and we needed to articulate this

Lean Begins With the Customer

Here are some fundamental questions and thoughts for your organization as you begin your Lean journey:

- What do your customers want?

- What do they value?

- What do your customers think of you as a company?

- When do you get feedback from customers?

- Do you get enough such information?

- Feedback must be routinely available on an ongoing basis.

strategy unambiguously to all our employees. It needed not only to get us out of our quandary, but also to drive the organization toward excellence, toward our vision. We needed a strategy that could be expressed in clear, unambiguous terms – something we could concretize, which employees could understand easily and pick up and run with.

Every strategy has to rest upon a few key pillars, and this is how Vlot built his. He established five key pillars for our new strategy, aptly named Up To Excellence:

The Up To Excellence Strategy

1. Planning, Tracking and Reporting
2. Process and Perfomance Improvement
3. Human Capital Development
4. Supplier Management
5. Support Innovations

The first pillar initially emphasized the establishment of a more reliable and accurate system of measuring performance and progress in all areas of our business. Timely and reliable reports would act as a dashboard from which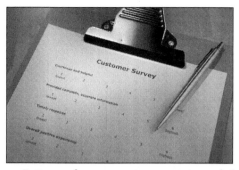

Better performance measures were needed

we could read our progress and steer the organization. This extended into a proper system of quarterly target setting and reviews, further expanded later on to include a top-down and bottom-up planning process to strengthen employee ownership, engagement and empowerment.

The next pillar, Process and Performance Improvement, included all the operational activities that we would undertake to drive change and improve processes using the Lean platform. Kaizen events were to be the key vehicles for executing changes to processes. Operation Breeze would be the organization-wide improvement project to drive us toward our goals. This would include all the intentional steps we needed to take, along with clear milestones on progress so that we could be sure we were progressing well and were on track to achieve our vision.

The third pillar concerned the development of human capital. CS&S needed a renewed emphasis on upskilling and upgrading its employees, including cross-skilling and opportunities for knowledge transfer. For a start we needed to inventory our employees' skill sets. Employee development plans were to be drawn up and executed. In conjunction with this, training opportunities had to be identified – all of this to quickly ramp up our human capital capabilities.

Good suppliers and solid working relationships with them are crucial to success in all organizations. Hence the fourth pillar of our strategy involved increased and renewed focus on supplier management. We had to focus on both internal and external suppliers. Close cooperative relationships were essential with Baan Development, our Research and Development arm which built the new products, and also PEG, which performed the software maintenance on the products.

PEG would be moved from the Baan Development organization and integrated into CS&S, but this required significant work to break down the existing barriers between PEG and Support. We needed closer ties with and increased assistance from Baan Development for the preparation of new product roll-outs, and for release control and management of new products.

Supporting all these four pillars was the last, comprising new or enhanced systems and methods which would reinforce the Lean platform, help us monitor our progress, assist us in decision-making, raise our capabilities for knowledge capture, retention, transfer and sharing, and provide us with additional operational strengths to meet the needs of our customers. Support Innovations was to be the last pillar.

These key pillars defined CS&S's forward direction, comprising our Up To Excellence strategy. Defining it in this manner enabled leaders at all levels of the organization to explain the strategy to employees simply and clearly, so they could understand it well and run with it.

Initiatives and tactics were then developed for each pillar in order to flesh out the strategy in executable detail. Every pillar had to embrace Lean thinking and principles, so that the performance improvement project could be driven powerfully. This also created the environment for a sustainable Lean culture to develop throughout the organization so that true transformation could take place.

It was imperative that *every* pillar, *every* initiative and *every* tactic was aligned with Lean principles. This was to ensure that no waste was created in the organization; that silo thinking was not reinforced, but instead broken down; that there was no reason for opposition to cooperative behaviour, but that teamwork was strongly supported and encouraged; and that there would be no cause for any un-Lean behaviour in the organization as a result of the new strategy, initiatives or tactics.

All the pieces had to come together and fit perfectly, every piece aligned. It was not enough to drive Lean without other pillars of the strategy being submitted to Lean thinking. Any un-Lean policy, activity or practice had to be brought into alignment.

The next chapter covers the vital step of communicating this new Up To Excellence strategy to employees, and how a crucial transformation event was used to drive home the message and win over a critical mass of middle managers. And so began our amazing journey . . . a journey of Lean transformation for CS&S.

LEAN PICKINGS

► Ensure your vision is clearly linked to measurable goals which employees can easily understand and relate to, so that it is evident when you have achieved your vision.

► Set aggressive goals for the organization: it is common to halve the problem, the issue or the waste in three to six months. Aggressive goals ensure two things. Firstly, the organization doesn't carry on doing 'business as usual', paying only lip service to the improvement drive, which will obviously not bring dramatic change or improvement. Secondly, they force managers and employees to think 'out of the box' and aggressively come up with novel and untried solutions in order to achieve the organization's goals.

► When the call backlog is cut the queuing time is reduced, which means that the average resolution time of cases in the backlog will fall. The key is therefore to concentrate on making improvements so that the case backlog can be reduced. Proactive measures should also be taken so that the incoming call volumes are reduced in the first place.

► There are two main drivers of average resolution time: the size of the backlog, and the quality of work output. Poor quality of work output causes the need for more re-work. Re-work adds to the case backlog and is waste, because the cases get re-opened and have to be worked on again!

▶ An organization's strategy should always be defined in clear and concretized terms so that employees can easily understand it and run with it. Every pillar, every piece of the strategy must be well defined and aligned to Lean thinking and Lean approach, not conflicting with it to create waste. This extends into every part of the organization – from the goals that are set, to the emphasis adopted for training programs, to how partners are treated, and onto how technology is selected for use by the operation.

7

ONE, TWO, THREE ... JUMP!

Robert Oh

*In which the leadership launches its
Up To Excellence transformation strategy and
convinces its management to take a leap of faith.*

BEFORE RETURNING FROM HIS TRAVELS TO visit key customers and major CS&S locations around the world, Ardin Vlot had already decided on his next actions. One by one he spoke to each member of the SLT team – individually at first, and then collectively – to explain the new CS&S vision and to ensure that a firm consensus was built as discussions proceeded. To ensure success he knew SLT members needed to get on board and run with the new vision and strategy.

Vlot also understood that within CS&S, as in all organizations, there were many talented employees, and that transformation would not happen by depending solely on a few excellent people; instead, we had to tap the talent and capabilities of the entire organization. We had to win the hearts and minds of the masses – every employee mattered, and each should have a stake. To reach this goal Vlot knew he first needed to reach every middle manager directly.

To achieve this he decided to launch CS&S's Lean journey with a transformation event for all the middle managers from around the world. He wanted this to happen within the next few weeks so that he could challenge and convince them of the urgent need for action and for the new vision and strategy. This was to be the first of several powerful transformation events targeted at middle managers enabling Vlot to communicate the urgency for change and to lead the charge towards reaching the new vision.

Vlot was keenly aware that organizations with the best results in transformation are often facing a crisis of some kind. So he knew he had to clearly communicate to middle managers the challenges CS&S faced. This was necessary to create that strong sense of urgency needed to fully mobilize them. If it was critical to obtain the buy-in of the SLT, it was even more vital to have middle managers get on board so that they could take the message down to the next levels, engage closely with their team members, explain and convince them of the urgency, and help them embrace this new vision and strategy.

The organization was soon abuzz concerning this global meeting. Much curiosity arose, and also much excitement. CS&S

Transformation Event

This is an event attended by senior and middle managers at which a coalition for change is established. This coalition must comprise a critical mass of managers who are won over to the new vision, strategy and goals so that a concerted effort can be made to drive and support the transformation effort across the organization. These events also serve as a means to enable the leader to communicate the urgency for change and to build esprit de corps across the entire management team to run the same race, in the same direction and towards the same goal.

HQ in Holland was a hive of activity – finding a suitable venue for the event, putting together the program, and sorting out all the details needed.

Not long after, more than 100 middle managers converged from around the world for the five-

Ardin Vlot knew he had to clearly communicate to middle managers the challenges CS&S faced

day event. It was a first for the CS&S organization, a major milestone. Nothing similar had been done before: the entire SLT and all the middle managers together in a single meeting! This was the platform used again and again to convince and win over middle managers – a clear example of going and reaching out to gemba. Vlot knew if he won their hearts and minds the rest would fall into place, and we would succeed.

After his welcome speech Vlot launched immediately into the challenges CS&S was facing. Customer satisfaction was low,

Aggressive Goals

It is typical in Lean enterprises to set aggressive goals. The usual initial target is to halve the problem within three to six months. Aggressive targets require and encourage new ways of thinking, new outside-the-box solutions. They also ensure that a high level of focus of attention and energy will be placed on the problem to resolve it. The alternative is a weak, perhaps half-hearted attempt to improve that will not result in significant gains.

and it was impacting sales; our case backlog was higher than it had ever been in the past. Serious and intentional measures were needed. We had to fight to keep our customers. The status quo could not be allowed to continue. We would use Lean transformation as the platform to cut waste, break down the walls between departments, improve productivity, and drive continuous improvement throughout the organization. And no time to waste, we had to get going immediately!

The huge call backlog was our most immediate challenge. Vlot told the meeting that we intended to halve it in six months!

Transformation Events

The thing that impressed me most was the transformation events. The first was held at Zandvoort – the first time all middle managers from the three regions had come together. At this meeting Ardin talked about the severe situation we were in and the need to turn the organization around. I clearly remember the feeling I had that finally something would be done.

Though no one spoke it aloud, there seemed a general acknowledgement of the problems we had, but also a sense that it was not possible to resolve them. As Ardin announced the launch of our Lean journey and explained how it would help us to reach the new vision, I believe I saw more and more managers become skeptical. During the break I heard several managers saying that the problems we faced were too big to tackle, and the situation would remain as it was no matter what we tried to do unless Baan Development could put out more stable software. I also heard them speak about past programs which had been tried and failed, or had resulted in only a short time of relief. I found this discouraging, because I had already begun to believe this Lean approach could really work.

During this event we were grouped into teams to work on the root causes of specific issues and subsequently come up with and present

Just prior to the meeting SLT members had worked out targets for call backlog reduction for every region and every support centre, right down to team level for the larger centres (including the PEG maintenance teams). Targets for each middle manager were issued to them that first morning of the meeting towards the end of Vlot's session. Right up front they all knew what their targets were, where their teams were at now, and where they had to get to.

These targets were released in this session to emphasize that Vlot and the SLT were not talking about some far-fetched

possible solutions. Each team continued to work on its plans after the meeting. It was the first time we ever had teams with members from all regions working together. This first meeting brought us together and created a strong sense of urgency.

After this we had several other transformation events in which we considered our progress against our goals, and shared success stories – what we had done and how we had achieved it. This inspired teams to learn from the successes of other teams and try out new things. Also during these meetings there was plenty of time to learn and strengthen our Lean skills. I really enjoyed playing a great game in which teams had to start up a company and trade with other teams, borrow funds, create marketing strategies, etc. It was aimed at turning us into entrepreneurs and empowering us to do what was necessary to provide new services to our customers.

Beginning with the first transformation meeting I saw a real turnaround in the organization, from a mentality of "No, we can't" to one of "Yes we can!" That new mentality unleashed enormous energy to drive improvement. I am really proud to have been a part of this turnaround, because now I know what it feels like to become a Lean organization.

Stefan Verbeek
Quality Project Manager CS&S EMEA

ideas and concepts for change. "The change starts now . . . and by the way, each of you has now received the targets you have to meet."

This was a new way of doing things. In the past middle managers had never been given operational targets involving such things as Backlog Reduction, First Time Right Rate of cases, or Average Resolution Time. The reality and enormity of the task hit home that morning. To help them achieve their targets, a series of initiatives founded on the new Up To Excellence strategy and Lean concepts and principles was to be launched – and employees would be empowered.

Employee empowerment and engagement were deemed crucial for success. A key principle of Lean says that employees who do the work should be the ones to identify and make the improvements. This is because they are the ones who are most familiar with their own work processes – and so that they are comfortable with the changes to those work processes, and will own those changes.

And so next on the agenda was the formation of eight groups of middle managers to match one-for-one the eight key issues

Strategic View from the Business Controller

It was a very positive change to see Ardin Vlot and his management team choose to drive Lean Transformation in the organization. The outcome of this program was not only improved processes but also increased productivity and customer satisfaction, as well as employee satisfaction. We achieved better revenue numbers and profit.

identified during Vlot's gemba visits to customers and CS&S support centres. To begin the empowerment process and put it into practice, each group was assigned one key issue to work on for its project (or kaizen) work. Each group was to brainstorm, understand the root causes, come up with ideas and solutions to fix the specific issues assigned to it, and then – importantly – to follow up on the implementation actions when the transformation event was over. With this project work began the empowerment of the CS&S organization.

The event turned out to be a resounding success. Middle managers caught the new vision and strategy, and a formidable coalition for change was shaped from that critical mass which is so vital to assure success and carry through a vision. A powerful momentum for change had been built. Almost every resistance to the new ideas and to Lean transformation had been demolished through careful convincing and reasoning. Step by step, all of the pieces required for success were carefully being put into place.

Most of the middle managers were truly glad something 'solid' had been fashioned. They had never been engaged like this be-

---

Ardin had a clear vision which was communicated to all the stake holders. All managers and employees were engaged and were given clear and realistic objectives which were measured, reported and reviewed on a regular basis. Business plans were implemented at all levels.

The deployment of Lean also provided me with additional responsibilities: Global HR and Global Human Capital Development Manager for CS&S. With Lean we expected to see more empowerment along with adequate but lesser controls, but instead what actually happened was we gained more 'control', because everyone now had better visibility of all ins and outs of both the financial and operational sides of the business.

Herman Steijger
Business Controller CS&S

Kaizen

Kaizen is a Japanese word meaning 'good change'. A kaizen is a continuous improvement team project typically involving between 5-7 employees. The goal of a kaizen project is often set aggressively, and must in almost all instances be measurable. Kaizens are meant to be rapid projects, the intent of which is to complete the project typically within 30 days from the kaizen event. This ensures that teams remain focused and the project is given the necessary work priority.

fore. There was a clear path ahead, and a clear philosophy to guide us. The end goals for us to reach our vision were clear. Understandable plans were now being implemented to reposition the entire CS&S organization, and these would help them solve many of the problems they faced with customers on a day-to-day basis.

This was the first major milestone in the transformation of the CS&S organization. The focus now turned to execution of the new Up To Excellence strategy. In the next several chapters we cover the development of each of the individual strategy pillars, the first of which addressed our ability to plan, track and report on the progress we were making.

LEAN PICKINGS

▶ A large coalition of like-minded leaders needs to be built to succeed in the transformation of an organization. The leader must take intentional steps to make this happen in both his own team and the middle management ranks.

▶ The Lean hardware – Lean tools and techniques – is a necessary ingredient for transformation to take place. But even more important is the software. You must win the hearts and minds of middle managers and employees concerning the vision, strategy and goals.

▶ Set clear goals. Communicate and cascade them down to middle managers and employees in such a way that teamwork across the organization is created and conserved at all levels of the organization.

▶ Empowerment requires clear direction and the setting of clear-cut boundaries so that employees know what to do and where their limits are.

▶ Take on a mode all across the organization that says "immediate action is required".

▶ Hold powerful transformation events to provide direction to the organization for its next steps going forward.

▶ The transformation events are to be used for creating informal networks and for strengthening working relationships between managers and peers. Interna-

continued

tional teams are set up to work on projects, and this will reinforce team work and team spirit across the geographies.

► Kaizens are to be completed within 30 days of the Kaizen event. Experience shows that when a project is not completed quickly it is often not successful. This is because of changes in work priorities, staff resignations or staff redeployments, and so on.

► If a project requires more than 3 months because of complexity reasons, the best approach is to break it down into several smaller projects or stages with shorter milestones. For every milestone define acceptance criteria, celebrate what you have achieved, and communicate this!

8

FOR GOOD MEASURE
Planning, Tracking and Reporting
Sunit Prakash

In which nothing is taken for granted any more,
and comprehensive analysis and measures of
performance are put in place.

A CLOSED LOOP PERFORMANCE MANAGEMENT SYSTEM had
to be built to keep Ardin Vlot and the SLT abreast of the
organization's progress, and part of this had to come in the
form of a management dashboard. How were we trending in
terms of our case backlog? What was the quality of solutions
delivered to customers, measured by the First Time Right
Rate? What was our Average Resolution Time for closing our
cases?

A team of two business analysts was immediately hired to begin work on building the management and reporting system.
Prior to this no such employee positions existed in the organization. This meant additional headcount positions were required, which may seem counter to the principles of Lean. On
the contrary, deploying Lean often means putting the right
resources into the right places to perform the right kind of
work.

In this case the additional hires were well worth the extra cost. The analysts examined our organization's whole business and determined what performance measures would be appropriate for us. They were also tasked to look into how these could be measured, and to establish their operational definitions so that they would be measured in a reliable and consistent manner. The operational definitions also ensured that a set of standard measurements was defined.

In addition, an appropriate business intelligence software tool had to be identified and deployed so that all senior and middle managers could have access to the performance measurement data that would be downloaded into the tool. This business intelligence system, aptly named Support Information System or SIS, would allow the data to be sliced and diced for data mining purposes. The system allowed any manager from any part of the world to examine and analyze the performance data of any team, any region – and he could also do the same for the entire global CS&S organization.

As training on the system began, its usefulness became clear to all. Each week managers and employees from around the world could glean information on their team's performance: quality of solutions, aging of cases, average resolution time of cases . . . just to name a few of the measures available. From here reports of all these performance measures could be plotted to show week-by-week trends.

The business analysts were soon busy revamping our detailed monthly operations report. This report summarized monthly performance for the organization and was circulated to the SLT. Now circulation was to be extended, reaching as far down the organization as possible (limited only by confidentiality restrictions of the report's contents). The financial information was enhanced, now including both the top line and bottom line information for each support centre and for each region, and a host of other indicators.

GLOBAL SCORECARD REPORTING TEMPLATE							
Scorecard		2002 Q3	2002 Q4	2003 Q1	2003 Q2	2003 Q3	2003 Q4
		Total Support					
Total revenue	[k$]						
COS Excl. transfer price	[k$]						
Total Overhead	[k$]						
Total cost	[k$]						
Contribution Margin	[k$]						
Contribution Margin %	[%]						
Total Headcount	[No.]						
Backlog	[No.]						
Backlog age	[Days]						
Resolution time	[Days]						
Lean Flow Ratio							
FTRR	[%]						
% Within 1 day	[%]						
% Within 5 days	[%]						
% Within 10 days	[%]						
Overall CS&S Performance							
Time to provide a solution	[Days]						
Quality of solution							
Referenceability	[%]						
CCFF rating/overall rating	[0-10]						
CCFF Satisfied	[%]						

Example of the scorecard template for consistent global visibility

Next, more customer satisfaction metrics were added to the monthly report. It was critical that we knew what to measure, and having a clear vision gave us really good guidance for this. A vision of Best In Class, translating to 'Customer Satisfaction Gap score of < 2.0', meant we had to focus on measuring the gaps in our customer satisfaction.

In addition we examined customer satisfiers. We discovered that customers were mostly interested in quality of the solution, timeliness of the solution and predictability of it – or our ability to meet our promise or commitment when we provided the customer with a promised solution date.

Quality was easily measured in terms of the First Time Right Rate, a common industry metric: the reciprocal of the number of ostensibly closed incidences or cases being reopened. But we also measured the emotional quality of the solution. Our support analysts may have fixed the problem, but did they 'fix the customer'? That is, was the customer satisfied with the solution?

For this we used a transaction-based measurement system giving the customer an opportunity to rate the solution once it was delivered. All customers who had logged a call at the point of receiving a solution from us were asked to rate our service through the internet. Admittedly this was not anonymous, but it worked well, and I see that Apple uses the same technique for their support.

In terms of timeliness, we measured Response Time and Resolution Time. Response Time was relatively easy, since it was generally an acknowledgement that the case had been received and someone from the support centre had now had a preliminary look at it and had assigned it to the most appropriate resource or support analyst. Once we understood that Response Time was a key customer-satisfier metric, it was easy to fix. We simply had to change our processes so that these cases did not sit unattended.

Resolution Time was a different matter altogether. By their very nature, many ERP-related cases are either complex functional issues or program bugs. Sometimes a vigorous debate would break out, and the product architect would need to be brought in to explain the intended functionality of the product design.

We set a measure of expectation here: something along the line that 99% of the cases would be resolved within five working days. Of course this was not always possible. Sometimes fixes would only be released in the next version or release; or sometimes customers' proposed way of using the product was not in line with the product.

No matter what, customers did not like to be left in the dark – "The Black Hole of Calcutta", as they called it. We improved our processes and systems so that customers could see the date and status of the bugs that went to the PEG. So in addition to resolution date and the target metric, we also had another key metric called Meeting Our Promised Resolution Date.

In the end our core set of metrics comprised customer satisfaction, quality of solution and timeliness – with some ancillary metrics that gave us clues and helped us manage the key metrics. Some of these ancillary metrics included:

- Helpfulness of technical personnel
- Clarity of support personnel's answers
- Technical skills of support personnel
- Ease of accessing support via phone
- Ease of accessing support via web
- Efficiency of case logging process
- Efficiency of web logging process
- Information contained in the support database.

The customer satisfaction surveys we had been making on a regular basis were now aligned to our requirements. With the metrics set, the next step was to understand what our current position was – the 'as is' picture.

Reports were generated so that we could see all the metrics at a global level. And in line with our organization structure, we could drill down and see the same metrics for each of our three international regions, and then drill down further to see the metrics not only per support centre, but also by queue for each support centre. The report also now included improved charts showing how we were trending against all the key customer metrics.

The SLT then set about doing some capacity analysis. Based on some esoteric logic, the number of heads, the average time to resolve a case, and the number of cases expected to be logged, quarterly global, regional and local targets were set.

Of course this took care only of the backlog. And I deliberately use the term 'esoteric', because to this day I do not understand how Vlot could say we would halve the backlog in six months without doubling the headcount! The Backlog Age, Customer Satisfaction, Resolution Time, First Time Right Rate etc. would only improve with improvements to our processes.

In hindsight I can see it was the power of a simple vision communicated well and supported by Lean process improvement and empowerment of the people closest to the process.

Nonetheless, the metrics comprised a simple and elegant spreadsheet that any support manager, team leader or support analyst could understand. They could see the actuals, the targets, how their performance directly affected global performance, and in turn the vision and mission – and so there was tremendous buy-in and support from the ground.

Vlot was on a call every week with a different support centre around the globe, going over the targets and performance with each support manager. He had a genuine desire to understand the issues and how roadblocks could be removed – I do not recollect a single call being punitive. Later, he would visit each support centre to see the progress they had made. This was essentially a management audit of sorts, a practice of going to the ground – to gemba.

We needed to put some context around the numbers. The detailed monthly operations report was revamped with the sales and consulting audience in mind in order to provide a commentary around performance and to highlight some of the issues.

The report started off with the global operational metrics, examining the details for each region. It also spelled out the performance of the PEG and their timeliness and backlog when it came to resolving defects. It went a couple of steps further. It listed 'escalated' customers, and customers with the highest amount of backlog. It also showed which versions and modules caused most cases to be logged. We could see at a glance that stable older versions had a declining number of calls, while newer versions, releases or modules that were being implemented at that time had a higher number of cases – and then the trending of those cases over time.

This took care of our operational targets, but it was not enough. Anyone running support knows that you have 'hot' or 'escalated' customers: that the number of incidences logged shoots up when there is a new implementation being performed, or if a new version of software is released. So we added a list of our top ten customers in terms of number of incidences logged.

In APJ we developed a regional scorecard, where, in addition to the key operational metrics, we also began keeping a score of additional revenues generated, and reporting on any ongoing initiatives and projects. It was a simple but effective balanced scorecard that gave in one page the total picture of what was going on and where we were at, and also the quarterly trend for each support centre in the region. Our weekly APJ conference calls were consequently focused, short and extremely effective.

We now had a total understanding of our business. We could tell what the issues were, where they were and whom they were impacting. We could tell how happy our customers were, or if they were not. We could clearly enunciate our vision and what programs of work we had in place to achieve it. Our support analysts evolved from being case-solving machines to beings of a higher level, proactively preventing problems and generating additional revenues.

Aside from the revamp of the monthly report, it was necessary to strengthen goal setting and performance review procedures. A new quarterly goal setting and performance review process was put in place. Targets were clearly tied to the quarterly bonus reward system. A top-down bottom-up planning process was also developed and implemented, the objective of which was to reinforce the cultural change taking place as employees came to feel more and more empowered in the organization.

In order to fully leverage the talent we had in the organization we had to develop our human capital to the fullest. This was the second of our strategic pillars – after all, the organization depended on people talent to make things better, whether it was improving processes or finding the best technology to leverage. In addition, to be able to work highly efficiently and effectively we needed to strengthen our skills and capabilities. We cover the development of human capital in the next chapter.

LEAN PICKINGS

► Build an effective measurement and reporting system that will provide timely, reliable and accurate information to support your management dashboard and use it to drive your business.

► Trending information is vital in your management reports and dashboards so that negative developments can be spotted and early action taken to correct such trends. Many companies have developed such management reports and dashboards, but for some, while the tools exist, they are not well used. For others, the information is not closely tied to goals that have been set in employee compensation systems. This makes the information interesting at best, for many of the managers and employees have no stake in whether the company goals are met or not.

► Deploying Lean often means putting the right resources into the right places to perform the right kind of work.

► Operational definitions of measurements are required to ensure that a set of standard measurements is defined to be measured correctly and consistently in the same way. All too often in companies, existing measurements have been misunderstood in terms of what they represent. The proverbial "I thought it represented . . ." happens way too often.

► The measurement for quality of work output is First Time Right Rate (FTRR), which refers to the percent-

(continued)

age of output that is complete and without errors the first time through. This is a key measurement, but is often difficult to obtain in real life. Where possible, automate the measurement of FTRR.

► The leader has to make a practice of going to the ground regularly to keep close, conducting direct observation to see and understand what actually happens. An audit plan is often developed to ensure this is carried out.

► Change compensation and reward systems so that they are closely tied to the accomplishment of your business goals at all levels. This is more easily said than done. While the benefits of doing this are understood, in almost all organizations I have come across it is deemed too difficult to change. No one wants to rock the boat.

► Top-down and bottom-up planning processes come into play to support the new culture of greater empowerment and higher engagement of employees.

9

PEOPLE POWER
Human Capital Development
Sunit Prakash

In which the organization learns to turbo-charge its people, and makes going to work more meaningful, challenging and fun.

FROM AN HR PERSPECTIVE, LEAN DEMANDED two things: empowerment, and dealing with the 'concrete heads'.

Our first step was to fill open positions and remove temps and contractors as far as possible. If we were going to upskill personnel, we might as well upskill our own people! It would be un-Lean to upskill personnel, release them at the end of the vendor contracts with us, and then have to re-hire and reskill once again.

Lean went deeper and deeper with training and workshops at each of the support centres. This was followed by kaizens. And once a kaizen was complete, more kaizens followed. There were local kaizens and global kaizens. A database of kaizen improvements was established to allow sharing of experiences and knowledge.

Each country support centre undertook a Lean self-assessment both to evaluate its current status against each element

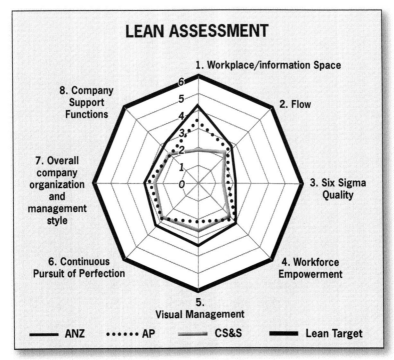

Spider chart showing Lean Assessment globally, and per region, and per centre (this chart was adapted from the book Lean Transformation *by Henderson & Larco)*

of Lean, and so that it could see what progress was made over time. The results were shown on a spider chart at each centre. Lean champions were appointed in every geographical region to coordinate and drive activities to make us leaner.

A key principle of Lean is that people closest to the process work to improve it. This is empowerment. This was the kind of environment we built, and with it came the results.

Once these two essentials are in place, empowerment will happen.

Change of this kind and magnitude does not happen without detractors. Although they were few and far between, Vlot dealt with the concrete heads so that he had 100% of his middle

Empowerment in Lean

If empowerment is to work in any organization, two essentials must be present. First, there must be clear direction arising from a clear vision and clear goals. Secondly, boundaries must be set. Ambiguities should be dealt with, and employees need to be informed of the limits to their empowerment.

management team on board with him. If even a small number of these managers were uncomfortable with or had difficulty accepting the vision, the change effort could be derailed.

One standout example of an improvement in a process had to do with 'linking solutions'. Lean demands 're-use'. Our support analysts found that they were often solving the same issue faced by many customers at many locations at the same time – but without the knowledge that many of them were working on the same thing. This was unnecessary re-work.

Interrogating the knowledge base was a hit-and-miss process trying to find similar cases, or (if the issue was already solved) to find the correct solution. Often the knowledge base held several versions of solutions.

The support analysts asked for an easy way to link similar cases to each other, and also similar cases to a given solution. This

Concrete Heads

Those who are unable or unwilling to accept the change in direction and the new vision and change their behaviour, are viewed as the most serious obstacles to a Lean transformation effort. In some instances, however, concrete heads eventually get turned around to become strong proponents of Lean.

was discussed, the system was modified and reports run. Soon the analysts were vying to have the greatest number of cases associated with a solution they had created! The solution knowledgebase grew and became a very effective tool.

As we stormed, normed, formed, and kaizened at our transformation events, it became clear that the causes of our customer dissatisfaction were rooted in the following facts:

- There was an enormous breadth of product to be supported – from Enterprise Resource Planning software through to software for Customer Relationship Management, for the Warehouse Management System, for Supply Chain Management and Product Data Management, for a variety of combinations of hardware platforms, operating systems and databases. This was compounded by the usual issues with localizations, multi-byte translations and customizations done by customers.

- Not every support centre necessarily had the skills to support the full breadth of products sold in that market; often the second- and third-level teams were in other dispersed geographical locations.

- Many of our support centres were relatively new, comprising young, less experienced support analysts.

You can imagine these showing up during discussions for root-cause problem analysis and our Ishikawa fishbone diagrams.

Ishikawa Fishbone Diagram

This is a root-cause problem analysis tool. Fundamentally a cause-and-effect diagram, the Ishikawa diagram shows various categories of causes, and for each category of cause it then shows the breakdown of all likely and potential causes of the problem.

There was no blanket answer to resolve these problems. Grand Rapids in the US and Ede in Europe, for example, had the good fortune to have both critical mass in terms of size and therefore skills and infrastructure, and also the bonus of close proximity to their region's PEG centre, as well as to the development teams.

In India, our Global Support Centre in Hyderabad had to deal with calls of every kind from all over the world. The rest of APJ suffered from the tyranny of time zone differences from the 'mothership' in Holland, where a large part of PEG was located. And Japan in particular suffered from both language and multi-byte issues.

So we developed a number of programs that made sense in each region. First of all, each of the regions identified the minimum skills required to support their customers. Every support analyst had an Individual Development Plan created so as to achieve this. In smaller centres in particular, cross-skilling was a big thing; every analyst was required to be able to support a module in the primary area of their skills, plus one more secondary module. Frequent knowledge-sharing sessions were held so that 'brain dumps' could occur and skill sets be ramped up in the shortest possible time.

Our Mumbai support centre instituted stand-up meetings at the start of each day. They would go over the issues outstanding from the previous day, outline the plan of action for the current day – and, most importantly, they would assign a 'buddy' to a junior support analyst who was stuck trying to resolve a particular issue.

Exchange programs worked well in the US and Europe where experts from the large centres would spend time at the smaller centres, or an inexperienced support analyst would spend time at one of the larger centres. In APJ, when we flew Netherland-based product experts into the region, the local support team's enthusiasm was so high they seemed to be sucking the knowledge out of our visitors' heads!

In my experience, good support analysts sweat blood to resolve an escalation and hate relying on overseas support if they know they have the capability to resolve the issue themselves. So they saw these visits as wonderful opportunities to make life easier for themselves and the customers they supported.

During one such visit, the senior Dutch support analyst carried out training on a module for support, and on the running of proactive health check reports. He did a couple of analyses for customers, and also presented at a user-group meeting. The value we got out of it was tremendous, and he too went back with a very positive view of what was happening in the region. We appointed him our 'ambassador' in Holland – and in this manner continued to build very strong relationships globally.

Collateral to this was that the global support team became a truly *global* support team. It was like a family, and even though there were close to 500 in the support organisation, no one was a stranger, no matter which part of the world they were

Releasing Control

What a journey it was! We began by getting everyone on board led by Ardin, the initiator, driver, and supporter of the Lean transformation journey, and ended up with an empowered CS&S organization pursuing excellence.

Empowering the teams was a big and kind of scary step for me. It required a significant change in management style. In the 'old' style you think you have conin. It is comparatively easy to accomplish this at a senior or middle management level on account of frequent travel and meetings; but we accomplished this at support analyst level.

We also found that when PEG or development teams specialising in one module were spread over more than one location, we had the issue of contention for system scripts and dlls which were being held by the particular PEG engineer working on a program until he completed his work. To resolve this we adopted the 'one domain one location' doctrine, so that all second-level support and development for a module was done in one single location, making for faster, easier support and development. This also enabled support analysts to understand the code better, while at the same time enabling the PEG engineer to appreciate customer issues better.

And finally, to top it all, we trained our support analysts in 'soft skills'. Analysts knew how to fix the technical problems; but sometimes, being analysts, they forgot about the customer. This program prepared them to be able to take care of both.

With the training and development of the support analysts and PEG engineers, and the breaking of barriers, a global net-

trol that you are going to lose in empowering the teams. In the end it is not about control but about getting the right results: giving excellent service to the customer. In that light I had to set the right goals and give the teams freedom to achieve them in the most effective way.

It was amazing to see the spinoff. Teams stepped up to the plate by becoming very innovative, taking responsibility, and fixing the problems they were facing. Work became fun. Managing became more transparent, focused and efficient, resulting in EMEA reducing from three to two layers of management.

Sonja de Feijter
Vice-President CS&S EMEA

work of trust developed. Coupled with process improvement, customer satisfaction improved astronomically.

Lastly, a mentoring scheme began. This was flexible, in that it allowed anyone to contact a senior person – and, if that person was willing, he would act as mentor to the support analyst or PEG engineer who contacted him. This supported even more networking across regions, leading to further improvements in cooperation. All of this added to the success of the Up To Excellence strategy.

The first strategic pillar, *Planning, Tracking and Reporting*, provided us with the ability to track and report on how we were progressing. The second pillar, *Human Capital Development*, focused on increasing the capability and skills of our employees and managers. The focus of the third strategic pillar, *Process and Performance Improvement*, was on the execution of process improvement, kaizen activities and project management of the organization-wide project Operation Breeze. In the next chapter we explore this further.

LEAN PICKINGS

► Establish a database of kaizen improvements to share knowledge and experience within each site and among sites. This will enable the new ideas and experience gained to be pulled by other locations for their use.

► Undertake a regular Lean assessment to capture a snapshot of where you are on your Lean journey. This helps your organization's departments and teams reflect on how Lean they are, and to track their own progress over time. If it is taken as a self-assessment, as far as possible it should be completed by the same group of individuals each time.

► Appoint Lean champions for each of your regions or sites.

► Deal with your concrete heads if they are unwilling to come on board.

► Emphasize training and cross-skilling and use creative methods like buddy systems, exchange programs, knowledge transfer sessions and concepts like 'one domain one location'.

► Adopt 'soft skills' training to complement technical skills.

10

OPERATION BREEZE
Process and Performance Improvement using Lean
Robert Oh

*In which every process is critically examined,
company culture is transformed,
and success breeds success.*

THE THIRD ASPECT OF OUR TRANSFORMATION, *Process and Performance Improvement,* was executed as an organization-wide improvement project titled Operation Breeze. 'Breeze' was a whimsical acronym for 'Backlog Reduction – Evolution to Excellence – Zillion Enjoyment'.

One of my earliest memories of Operation Breeze was of flying into Holland in mid-2000 for the quarterly meeting of the SLT and, after reaching the office, finding that Ardin Vlot wanted to bounce several of his ideas off me. He asked for my commitment to support his initiative to try to halve the backlog, and he spoke about the idea of having a transformation event which he called a Middle Management Meeting. It was a lot to take in after my 13-hour flight!

I liked the idea of a transformation event, but was wondering exactly which middle managers would be involved. If it was just going to be a few, I thought it wouldn't have much of an impact. . . .

I don't remember if Vlot spoke about Lean at that meeting. I think he probably did, but I can't remember for sure. Lean was still really new to me. I actually found *Lean Transformation,* the book which all the SLT members were given, quite difficult to read.

On the week after returning from that meeting in Holland, I remember being on our regular SLT conference call. We were once again discussing as a team how our backlog reduction goal needed to be aggressive. We would halve the backlog in six months!

Baan's case backlog had never been higher than at that time – 10,000 open cases! I knew that all previous efforts to cut our backlogs had never been successful, no matter what initiatives we had tried. So while we were deciding as a management team to shoot for a drastic cut in the backlog, some doubts lingered in my mind: How on earth were we going to do this? We had never been successful in the past – why would we be successful now? What was going to be different this time around?

As these thoughts raced through my mind, I also wondered who would have to lead this global performance improvement effort. I thought of Sonja de Feijter, the new Vice-President of Support for EMEA . . . no, not likely – she was new to the team. She had just transferred to CS&S from the consulting organization in Holland. It wasn't likely to be me, I thought, because I led the smallest region of the three. So I concluded that Ken Crossman would get the job.

Over the phone Vlot was getting everyone's agreement and commitment to the aim of cutting our backlog by half within six months. Then he suddenly said, "Robert, I would like you to lead this project." I couldn't believe my ears! Frankly, I was

> ## Visual Management
>
> A Lean tool used for the purposes of communicating visually. It enables employees to see a 'bigger picture' and is intended to provide immediate feedback on the status of an operation. The means of communication is visual and non-verbal, often using visual cues of some kind and allowing visual control of an operation to take place.

shocked – it was a good thing no one could see me, since I was at the other end of the line in Singapore. However, this moment began the most exciting years of my working life.

Having been assigned this task I got to work immediately. I was to build a project plan for Vlot to review, and I wanted to make sure we had clear steps to take to bring us through the initial six months to where we wanted to be.

This also included beefing up the support strength at Hyderabad, the Global Support Centre supporting all the three regions. This was the lowest cost option to raise headcount and help clear some of the backlog – but we needed experienced people who could immediately be deployed to contribute to reducing the backlog. So I asked for additional 'temp help' for Hyderabad Centre, to be recruited from our Indian partners.

At the first transformation event in Holland, Vlot rallied the support of all the middle managers as he articulated the need for things to change and explained that the organization would embrace Lean as a culture and a tool to help us get there. On one of the evenings during this meeting, everyone took a stroll along the shores of Zandvoort wearing a jacket with *Operation Breeze* on its back to commemorate the beginning of our journey together. It was a breezy and cold evening, but it was a very memorable event.

Because of my military training I knew that if we were to succeed – and we had to succeed! – we needed to be absolutely focused. So when Vlot requested that I put out a weekly update on progress, I jumped on it. The progress updates were targeted at both our internal customers (Sales & Consulting) and our employees worldwide; they had to be succinct in delivering their message, and also had to motivate our employees.

A further purpose of these weekly updates was to raise the profile of this project, making it highly visible and creating a heightened state of awareness of how it was progressing with respect to its goals. With rapid feedback on progress our teams and regions could rally together and respond quickly to circumvent any weakness or shortfall we had, and take the necessary actions to get back on track. So it was important that every employee in CS&S could plainly see how we were progressing.

As Operation Breeze commenced, the communications to both our external and internal customers began. Customers were informed of our new vision, what our new strategy looked like, and our plans for Operation Breeze. We were sticking our necks out. We were not going to do Breeze and keep quiet

Root Cause Analysis: Reducing Support Cases Arising From Implementation

I recall using a root cause analysis to discover that a significant percentage of customer cases resulted from mistakes, omissions, or choices made during the software implementation phase. I polled several people across the regions for inputs, and together we drew up a series of actions that Support should take at key points during the implementation process. We aligned the implementation process (which was known as Target Methodology) with this list of actions by adding some new mile-

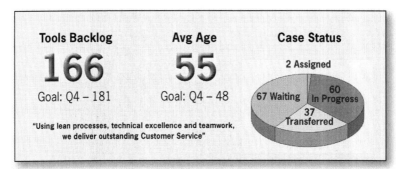

As an example of Visual Management, the team in Grand Rapids created a desktop ticker showing real time performance

about it. By communicating it widely to our customers and our internal customers in Baan we were committing ourselves and our organization, we were putting our personal reputations on the line, making failure not an option!

If we had been quiet and kept a low profile about our plans, we would have lacked the commitment needed, and we would have failed. Instead, we took every opportunity to tell our customers, our partners and sales operations about the new strategy and about Operation Breeze. We presented our vision and our plans during customer seminars and conferences, at user group meetings, and at other customer gatherings. We

stones. We then created a closed feedback loop that kept this list of actions dynamic as we learnt more, with an activity at the end that required any new learnings to be incorporated.

The idea was that as we encountered new or hidden causes that increased the number of support cases originating in the implementation phase, they would cause us to learn and update the activities list worldwide.

Matthew Loxton
Enterprise Support Manager AM

did road-shows to bring our good news to our customers and to sales offices in the various regions and countries.

Work began immediately. Kaizens here, kaizens there and kaizens everywhere. All hands were on deck, every employee in CS&S started to run while closely watching our progress.

At first when we began there was a degree of skepticism: "How can we achieve this?" "We've never been successful in bringing down the backlog before, no matter what we tried. What's the difference now?" But skepticism quickly turned into surprise when the backlog actually began to fall, albeit slowly. Not much, but there was a visible trend. This was encouraging, and served to create further impetus to drive for even more improvement.

The initial feeling of skepticism then gave way to a solid belief that we could actually do this. So we went for it, every employee running together in the same direction, in the same race, towards the same goal. The improvements began to snowball, and there was no stopping after that! The momentum for improvement just kept growing.

As we continued to improve, we freed up resources. This in turn meant we could put even more resources into the improvement effort. It felt surreal as every week the backlog reduction trend continued. After six months of tireless effort the backlog was indeed cut by 50% to a level we had never been able to achieve before in the history of our company. This was a great achievement, a deserved reward for all the efforts of CS&S employees!

When we reached our target, we celebrated. Vlot wrote a personal letter and sent it to every employee in CS&S, together with a trophy of a panther with the word 'Breeze' on it. The trophy captured the story, the events and the efforts that led to such a dramatic reduction in the backlog of cases. All around the world CS&S celebrated this win.

After Operation Breeze was over, we kicked off Breeze II as a continuation of our efforts. As we continued to cut our backlog our resolution times became shorter, and customer satisfaction shot up.

We kept considering issues from many different angles. We targeted the tough cases, what we called 'hard clay'. We went after specific modules of the software that were showing more issues than others. We looked at various means to help customers use more of the self-help tools. We started providing training to customers on using the web knowledge base. A software installation tool was developed so customers could now install patches in a more orderly fashion, and we began to provide onsite services to help customers optimize use of their software.

For customers who were less proficient, we began to handle patch installation for a fee. This increased our revenues while simultaneously reducing the incoming customer calls! Patches were released more frequently so that they could get to customers more quickly and so reduce incoming calls. We reduced interruptions by minimizing the number of high priority requests we allowed to interfere with any ongoing work. This raised productivity significantly. We looked at our processes and redesigned them to cut out any waste that we could find. We looked for ways to decrease re-work.

We changed our customer handling processes to ensure customers would be regularly informed of the status of their cases. We improved our performance relating to promised solution dates. We closely tracked the customer feedback we received, both through our regular customer satisfaction surveys and through the transaction-based surveys which we called the Customer Case Feedback Form (CCFF).

Whether a CCFF review was good or bad, we contacted the customer. If we received a compliment we called to express our appreciation. If the feedback was negative we called to find out more, so as to learn from our mistakes. Many kaizens ran in each of the regions, all targeted to help achieve CS&S's goals. All this meant our backlog of cases continued to fall.

Weekly updates kept CS&S employees constantly abreast of how we were progressing with the backlog, as well as a number of other key indicators. These updates were sent to the whole CS&S organization and our internal customers every week without fail, rain or shine, so as to maintain Operation Breeze's high visibility and keep everyone's minds focused on our goals. This is a prime example of the use of a Lean tool known as Visual Management. Below is an excerpt from one such update, the first one for the year 2002, sent to encourage all the teams after fifteen months of Operation Breeze. Each full update would always contain key metrics (Backlog, FTRR, etc.) along with end-of-quarter targets.

SITUATION REPORT

It's been a very eventful year... We had undertaken a real solid and focused effort with Operations Breeze 1 and as a result of that, by the end of March 2001, we managed to reduce our case backlog by 50%. This was by itself a major milestone for us back at that time. We did not stop there, and we continued to push even further onwards. More progress was made with Operations Breeze II throughout the year. Again this was by constantly improving our processes, strengthening co-operation, increased internal networking, greater empowerment and driving Lean Transformation at 'full force'. We made a significant break-through at the end of December, by achieving our backlog target and reducing backlog to close to a third of what it was when we had started to drive the backlog down. We will now once again continue to progress 'Up To Excellence'.

Operations Breeze II Committee
Robert Oh – Sonja de Feijter– Ken Crossman – Ardin Vlot

Part of a weekly email update on Operation Breeze (Week 1 of 2002)

Everywhere teams worked on kaizen projects to make things better every day, all the time. Continuous improvement in the true sense of the phrase was happening throughout the CS&S organization. Each week after I reported overall progress on Operation Breeze during our CS&S SLT calls, Vlot would review the numbers for each region and request action plans for areas that were not progressing well.

As we progressed with Breeze, we kept an eye on our other numbers. If we were going to shoot Up To Excellence, customers would benefit. Selling our customers support and maintenance – and collecting payments from them – would become easier. We could expect our revenues to continue to rise. The focus on managing contracts would continue. With fewer customer escalations, support managers could spend more time pursuing contract renewals and selling extended services. Operation Breeze was good for business.

Operation Breeze and Lean were never seen as extras – they were part and parcel of our daily work. Every week we worked, we ate, we slept, we dreamed Breeze and Lean. The project meetings and discussions over kaizen efforts in the regions were always a normal part of the weekly CS&S senior management meetings. In fact, to Vlot's credit, this topic was always placed first in the agenda on our weekly SLT conference calls, thus giving it first priority among all the topics discussed. There is much to learn from this simple but powerful approach to leading change.

At every location I visited during this period I would motivate the employees by reminding them that it was unlikely that they would ever find themselves in another organization where improvements and progress for a change effort happened so quickly and so dramatically, on such a large scale. We were literally history makers.

SITUATION REPORT

Congratulations to all teams! At the end of week 52 (week ending 27th Dec 02), we had already achieved our yearend backlog target of 2041 by coming in at 1959 cases!!!.

We also want to continue to sustain the gains in our backlog that we have fought so hard to get to. The importance of this cannot be overstated. So lets' cap the backlog as much as possible. It would be a disservice to all our teams (and ourselves) because of all the hard efforts that have gone in to bring the backlog down, to allow the backlog to again go back up to the levels we had 4 or 5 weeks ago. So lets' keep the pressure on and wind blowing...

With the turn of the New Year, we would like to wish one and all, and your families, a Happy, Prosperous and Wonderful New Year, as well as Good Health. This year may we get an even stronger wind (read as 'Breeze') beneath our wings, to carry us further on 'Up To Excellence'.

Operations Breeze II Committee
Robert Oh – Sonja de Feijter– Ken Crossman – Ardin Vlot

Part of the weekly email update on Operation Breeze 12 months later dated Week 1 of 2003

In January 2003 an update to Operation Breeze (above) was put out, showing the tremendous progress made as a result of the entire CS&S organization's worldwide focus on reaching our vision.

Along with backlog reduction and increasing customer satisfaction, Average Resolution Time continued to improve through the entire Breeze and Breeze II period. Beginning at 41 days in Q3 of 2000, the Resolution Time fell to just a quarter of this over the next 24 to 30 months.

We had all the right ingredients in place. We had an inspiring vision and clear, cascaded goals tightly linked to reward systems. We chose to make this change effort highly visible to all around, sticking our necks out since our internal customers all knew about our change efforts and progress, and our external customers had all been informed about Breeze and had been

Robert Oh with Benny Teng, the APJ Contract Manager who was instrumental in building the APJ contract database, went to gemba, and worked with APJ Support Managers to track all the new and renewal support contracts

promised significant improvements. We had absolutely no option but to succeed.

I believe pride was also a key success factor: pride in ourselves, and pride in our organization, CS&S. Employees all felt this pride, and no one was ready to let us fail. We had to succeed, and we did!

In order to ensure success we needed help from the back end of our value chain upstream from CS&S: our internal and external suppliers. We needed a strong and close working relationship with them. Because this was crucial it formed the next pillar of our Up To Excellence strategy, dealt with in the next chapter.

LEAN PICKINGS

▶ Execute the drive towards excellence as an organization-wide performance improvement project, with clear actions and steps to be taken and clear milestones to achieve.

▶ Ensure you get firm commitment from your team.

▶ As you go, create a heightened state of awareness concerning how the organization is progressing.

▶ Inform your customers and partners about your strategy and the actions that will be taken to bring the expected improvements. In other words: stick your neck out if you want to be successful!

▶ Make sure you celebrate your successes. The organization celebrates and not just the kaizen teams!

▶ Find all the waste you have in the organization and eliminate it.

▶ Make continuous improvement a way of life.

11

UPGRADING THE SUPPLY VALUE CHAIN
Supplier Management
Sunit Prakash

*In which relationships with suppliers are redefined
for the benefit of customers.*

LIKE ANY OTHER ORGANIZATION, CS&S HAD its suppliers.
Development was our supplier: they built the software and in
the past they had fixed the code, fixed the software bugs and
released the software patches. So one of the first changes that
took place when Ardin Vlot was given his new appointment
to head CS&S was that the maintenance organization in Baan
Development, the Research & Development arm of Baan,
became a part of CS&S.

To ensure good cooperation and strong ties remained with
Baan Development, Vlot needed someone who both understood the maintenance business well and also knew and had
strong relationships with all key Baan Development managers. He found this in Gert den Hertog, who led the new maintenance department of CS&S, called Product Engineering
Group (PEG).

It was vital for the support centres to be closely plugged into PEG, and equally, further upstream, PEG had to be well connected into the Development organization. We found that support analysts had good understanding of customers' issues, but had limited knowledge of the program code of the software modules. On the other hand, the PEG engineers knew the code well but did not always understand customer issues.

Customer feedback indicated that they were often not happy with certain types of advice they received. They no longer found the "try this patch and then get back to us" approach acceptable, and were demanding changes. In addition, support analysts often would not, and could not, advise customers when an issue would be resolved if it went past them to PEG.

Several key initiatives were taken. The first was to have PEG engineers sit beside support analysts to work on and resolve issues together. This concept, which came to be known as 'One Domain, One Location', opened up a whole new world to the PEG engineers, who now gained a deeper appreciation of customer problems and began to see things more and more from a customer perspective. In working with the PEG engineers, support analysts' understanding of the program code also improved.

To serve the customers better, knowledge sharing was crucial

A second initiative followed this one. PEG engineers were requested to actively pass on their knowledge of the program code to support analysts through briefings and so on. The support analysts' understanding grew to such an extent that in some cases they were now even able to code the bug fixes themselves and

Checklists

One of several Lean tools used for the purposes of mistake proofing. Checklists are often used to ensure completeness of activities, items or information, and they are often also used to ensure correct procedural sequence is used in a process.

provide them to the PEG engineers concerned, so the bug fix development time could be shortened.

Furthermore – increasingly, in severe customer situations – PEG engineers would fly into customer sites to assist customers together with the support analysts. The PEG organization began to undergo a metamorphosis of sorts, turning from its original more conservative culture into a highly customer-oriented organization.

The same was happening with Baan Development. A new product release process was installed to close the gap with Development for new product launches. This included a Known Error database, documentation, test systems, technical escalation procedures and training before support would 'certify' that the product was ready for release. In hindsight this looks elementary, yet at the time – with organizations needing to move with speed and agility – it was easy to overlook the readiness of support for new product launches.

Service level agreements were set up with Development, committing them to work on and commit resources to customer issues for new products launched – in this case the new Baan V product. Increasingly, cooperation between CS&S and Development strengthened. So throughout the value chain upstream from the support centres, we began to see significant changes and improvements commensurate with the advances being made within CS&S.

At one of our global kaizens we were exploring the root cause of our backlog of cases. We noticed a spike in calls when the customer was implementing and about to 'go live', or when a new version or release came out. So at local support centre level we began engaging with consulting services and implementation partners early in the implementation. We wanted no surprises, and put together a go-live checklist to weed out possible issues so that nothing would be missed.

The transformation events which began in the third quarter of 2000 and continued every half year involved PEG middle managers. They were an integral part of CS&S. In addition, some key Baan Development managers were also invited to these meetings. The meetings facilitated the development of informal networks throughout CS&S and Baan Development as these managers from various parts of the world got to know each other, worked in teams together, built friendships and, importantly, built trust.

Now when help was needed one had only to pick up the phone or send an urgent email and this help was assured – a far cry from the way it used to be in the past. Previously the organization had operated to a degree in silos – without a sufficiently clear vision, and certainly without enough cooperation. Things had now changed distinctly and positively. In the first place there were far fewer escalations and urgent customer issues. Where there were, all the parties engaged to support each other.

With this new state of affairs, CS&S's leadership now had time to plan, make improvements and dream of what to do next. Meanwhile the organization was also scrutinizing its global support infrastructure.

LEAN PICKINGS

▶ Bring backroom personnel closer to the customer to help them better understand the customer's perspective.

▶ Break down silos in the value chain to increase cooperation and teamwork.

▶ Support and facilitate the buildup of informal networks across the value chain, since this helps eradicate the silo mentality.

▶ Draw up cooperative service level agreements to increase cooperation and commitment.

12

BEHIND THE SCENES
Support Infrastructure, Innovation and Technology
Sunit Prakash

*In which technology improvements under the hood
make the ride smoother and more powerful.*

WHILE INDIVIDUAL TEAMS WERE BUSY IDENTIFYING 'boulders to break', executing kaizens and generally improving processes, CS&S also turned its attention to the fifth pillar of its Up To Excellence strategy: the need to examine and upgrade its global support infrastructure. Even without Operation Breeze infrastructural changes would have been required. Executing them at the same time meant that process improvements and system changes went hand in hand to support the overall strategy, resulting in quantum gains.

The most significant change was probably the renewal of the support website. Customers had always been able to log a case online and look at its status. Now a new feature was added, enabling them to load their profile and preferences and have solutions sent to them proactively – a quantum leap forward at the time!

Another key improvement was the introduction of a new knowledge base engine, followed by cleanup of the solution knowledge base. Support analysts often found in the knowledge base more than one solution to an issue, created by different individuals; many outdated solutions also remained accessible. There was no clear review pathway for approving solutions for publication once they were written and before they were posted to the knowledge base. Something clearly had to be done.

Module owners were appointed to review solutions whenever they were written up, before they could be accessed by support analysts or customers. Simultaneously, teams were organized to review all existing solutions, to remove extraneous solutions, and to clean up the knowledge base completely. While this activity took precious resources away from fixing customer issues, it clearly began to pay off quite soon after the effort was made.

Support analysts now found correct solutions for customer problems more often. This meant an improvement in First Time Right provision of solutions, and a reduction in wasteful re-work. Even better, more and more solutions could be placed in public mode, making them available to customers to download directly. By doing this we were able to reduce incoming calls to the support centres, further freeing up our support analysts to work on more important issues.

Another key development arising from a global kaizen had to do with Promised Resolution Date. The Case Management system was tweaked and a field added so that customers could see the status of defects that were with PEG. The Promised Resolution Date (PSD) now gave customers an indication of when they could expect the bug-fix to be available, rather than leaving them in the dark.

The introduction of the PSD field proved a major milestone in further satisfying our customers. A natural outcome from its introduction was the need to track how often PEG missed their PSDs. There was now increased focus to be on time – that is, 'just-in-time every time'.

One of the primary reasons why PSDs were missed was because of interruptions to the development of the

There was increased focus to pull cases and be 'Just in Time' every time

bug-fixes, due mostly to higher priority requests coming in for other bug-fixes. These requests could come from any customer and from any support centre, from any part of the globe. How was PEG supposed to respond when this happened? Who was going to decide the priority ranking of the various requests?

We determined that our three support regions would best represent customers' interests, and would have to prioritize the requests. We established a regular global escalation meeting involving the support regions and PEG which worked tirelessly to set the priority of defects to be fixed on a global basis. This meeting continued until 2003, by which time the number of customer escalations diminished to a level where it was no longer required.

The computer telephony integration platform Apropos was another significant implementation, giving us the ability to perform skills-based and time-based call routing. Our 24-hour Global Support Centre in Hyderabad did not necessarily have sufficient skills to support all variations of the ERP package, particularly if serious escalations came in after normal working hours. So it was decided to implement a 7x24 follow-the-sun support model, routing calls to Grand Rapids, Denver, Sydney and Ede outside Hyderabad's working hours.

We implemented a time recording system to track activity at the support centres. Online forums were also established as a means to discuss issues and technical solutions. These were an effective medium to share experiences and retain knowledge within the organization.

A web-based system serving as a database of all kaizen activity was set up, complete with search capability. This enabled support centres to review what others had done for their kaizen projects, and what their experiences had been. It supported a 'pull' of other support centres' ideas and best practices, which was certainly more effective than 'pushing' such best practices.

In many organizations the pushing of best practices results in parts of the organization resisting the change, insisting that their operations are not quite the same and that the best practices do not really apply to or benefit them. Instead of pushing the new ideas, we felt it was better to let interested parties pull them from the database. After all, to achieve their goals each of the support centres had to improve their operations significantly, which meant they had to be open to many of the fresh ideas coming from other support centres. Providing a search facility with the database supported this need to find new ideas for improvements.

All these improvements were of course designed to serve the purpose of increasing our 'customer happiness'. Increasing customer satisfaction was a clear signal that we were progressing. It was important for us to be able to obtain timely and accurate feedback on our customers' level of satisfaction. In the next chapter we turn our attention to what we measured to obtain this feedback, and how we did this.

LEAN PICKINGS

▶ Install proper knowledge management processes to ensure information integrity of your knowledge bases.

▶ Provide customers with as much information as possible so that they are informed of the status of their cases.

▶ Reduce interruptions to work to decrease setup productivity losses.

▶ Set up a kaizen database to support the pulling of solutions and ideas.

13

MEASURING CUSTOMER SATISFACTION

Sunit Prakash

In which better metrics enable the organization to focus on making its customers happy.

IN ORDER TO ACHIEVE BEST IN Class customer satisfaction, we engaged customer satisfaction survey specialists Prognostics. Our support centre in Grand Rapids already performed a regular CAT (Courtesy, Accuracy and Timeliness) Scan. Now Prognostics was commissioned to survey our customers' satisfaction in a more consistent and global manner.

An extract of all customers logging calls with Baan CS&S was made once a quarter and forwarded to Prognostics. Prognostics sent out to those customers a web-based questionnaire measuring a dozen or so attributes of service quality. Care was taken not to survey the same customers repeatedly in order to avoid survey fatigue.

Most customer satisfaction surveys ask customers to rate the service delivered, eg: *On a scale of 1-10, where 10 is the best, how do you rate the service provided?* This survey was different. While it asked the customer how they rated the service provided, it also asked how important that attribute was to the

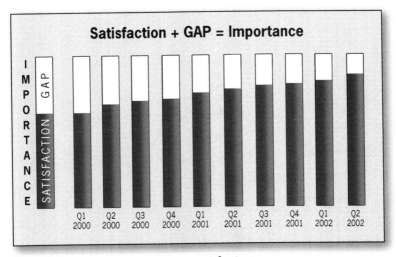

Chart showing increasing customer satisfaction

customer, or how the customer would ideally like that particular attribute to rate.

So a customer may say timeliness was rated at 6.5, but would ideally like that attribute to rate at 9.5. The gap between customers' expectations and the actual rating was the key metric of interest to us. In the same manner, in addition to individual attributes, the survey also measured the customer's overall satisfaction gap with the service.

Prognostics told us that if the gap was greater than 4, customers would walk away from us if they had a choice. On the other hand, if the gap was less than 1, then as a company we were probably over-investing. To get to Best In Class, then, our task was to reach a gap rating of 1.5 or less. This was easily measured, easily communicated, and very easily understood by the support staff, customers and other internal departments of Baan.

A direct result of this was that support staff were now able to see problem areas from a customer's perspective, and how their actions – including process improvement – made a clear impact on customer satisfaction. We examine staff empowerment and engagement more fully in Chapter 14.

Very quickly it became evident that the customer was only interested in two main things: getting the solution that fixed the problem first time, and getting it fast. So timeliness and accuracy (or quality) of the solution were the key elements.

We were also picking up survey comments made by our customers which gave us important clues to some of the underlying issues. This, along with comments made at user group meetings and employee inputs, helped us identify suitable candidates for kaizen improvement sessions. The Black Hole of Calcutta and The Promised Resolution Date, described in the next chapter, were examples of such kaizens.

As regular survey reports began showing us trending information, Lean principles were applied even to customer satisfaction reporting! In general, the smaller the batch of survey reports supplied, the shorter the turnaround time. APJ didn't want big batches of survey reports sent to us one quarter in arrears. We demanded immediate reports complete with customer comments. This enabled us to understand the causes of dissatisfaction and address them very quickly – before the end of the quarter, and before final survey results came out.

This sense of urgency was overpowering, and the results were very satisfying. Customers saw that we were not an anonymous global bureaucracy – we were turning into a lean, agile and responsive organization that listened to its customers.

In addition to the quarterly Prognostics survey, we also gave customers a chance to rate our service for each case logged with us every time they accepted the solution and closed the case. This was called the Customer Case Feedback Form (CCFF). It was quite brutal, and gave the support analyst immediate feedback on how customers felt their issue was handled. It wasn't anonymous, and our customers weren't shy about it either!

As key operational metrics including Backlog, Backlog Age, Resolution Time and First Time Right Rate were measured to track our internal performance, other customer satisfaction-related metrics like CCFF and the Prognostics Gap helped us to track our performance as evaluated by the customer.

The SIS system we set up included all the operational metrics plus the CCFF measurements. A download of the data gave us a relatively simple Excel sheet which consolidated global data for each of the metrics above. These included the actuals, but, more importantly, there were quarterly targets for each as well.

CS&S GLOBAL TARGETS		Average	Actual	Targets		
		Q1	Wk13	Q2	Q3	Q4
Weekly customer input	[# cases]					
Weekly customer output	[# cases]					
Backlog	[# cases]					
Lean Flow Ratio (LFR)						
Resolution time	[in days]					
Backlog age	[in days]					
80% solved within ... days	[in days]					
CCFF Satisfied	[%]					
CCFF Rating	[0-10]					
First Time Right Rate (FTRR)	[%]					
Nett capacity	[FTE in days]					
Productivity	[#cases/FTE/day]					

A view from the Support Information System (SIS)

Each of our three international regions could drill down from global targets. Each region could be further differentiated: for example, APJ could drill down to Japan, Korea, Greater China, Singapore, Malaysia, Australia/New Zealand and India. Each country could drill down further to team level.

So every support team around the world could see its performance and its target using the SIS system. It could see how its team was doing, how its support centre was doing overall, how its region was doing, and how we were doing globally!

In the APJ region we set up a scorecard that included the metrics above, together with some of the projects and initiatives we were rolling out. We then used the scorecard to run our weekly team meetings at a local and regional level.

Vlot had picked up pretty early on that our language and metrics were not consistent. If he asked a support centre manager what his backlog was, he would get a number. But the way Ede might calculate its backlog number would be different, for example, to Hyderabad or Barcelona.

There were also some games that support analysts and support centres played. Transferring cases to Hyderabad to reduce the local backlog was a hot favourite. This happened especially for the 'old smelly ones' – ie, the very difficult ones which had been outstanding for quite some time. Some support analysts were too quick to report having provided a solution and closed the case, when in fact only a tentative solution like "try putting on the latest service pack and see what happens" had been provided! As we journeyed on, all of this changed and transformation came.

The SIS tool helped us by making calculations, metrics and language globally consistent and standard. This was essential for a global organization.

Many of the actual process improvements were made by executing kaizens – an excellent vehicle for employee engagement. The principle of allowing those closest to the process to make the improvements to the process produced tremendous results as employees everywhere stepped up to participate in kaizens. They raised new ideas, suggested changes and improvements to existing processes, and also took ownership of these changes – all of this in order to achieve our goals. The

Value from a Customer's Perspective: How the Deal was Won

In my early years in the Customer Service and Support field one particular customer experience left an indelible impression on me.

My predicament began with a complicated customer situation in which the customer's maintenance renewal was due. The renewal amount was in the USD six-digit range and attracted management attention. The challenge was compounded because the customer was using a very old version of the software, demanded support for it, and would not upgrade since they had made a decision to move away to another software package. The customer perceived no value in renewing maintenance, making the discussion rather difficult – in fact, the customer wanted to terminate the maintenance contract. It was during this period that the customer hit a snag with their database, making an upgrade of the software inevitable. However the customer did not find value in performing a full-fledged software upgrade and, with these constraints in place, asked me to find a way to fix the issue.

Keeping in mind the potential renewal revenue at stake, I pulled together a multi-disciplinary team comprising R&D, consulting, support, and the customer's own technical resources, to create an 'outside the box' solution to solve their problem. The solution worked and the customer's problem was resolved. The support renewal which previously had looked overwhelmingly difficult now looked possible. The customer asked me to come over to their office for discussions.

next chapter describes more about the kaizens we ran, and how they were used to pursue improvements.

After a long day with several rounds of meetings, it was 7.00pm when their CIO called me to his room to take a look at the final offer. But the ghosts of a strained past commercial relationship continued to lurk, and soon I was putting my papers and the unsigned contracts back into my bag and about to leave. Unexpectedly the CIO stopped me and asked me to return the agreements to him. He said he would commit to renewal and would pay us within 15 days. Then he said, "Noel, this is just for you. You have worked hard to manage our account despite the challenges, you have shown us value. We appreciate your efforts and for this we will give this contract to you." I was overjoyed and walked out with my head high. As I walked out it became more evident to me that customer service and support, like all other services, is about creating value.

This creation of value arises from Lean Thinking. Lean Thinking revolves around 3 Ps: Purpose, Process and People. It is a process of continuous improvement aimed at eliminating waste along the supply chain and producing what is needed with the customer in mind. Customers are sensitive to your actions and interested in what you are going to bring to them to help make them successful in the businesses they engage in.

Lean is a journey and does not end with one particular transaction. It is continuous improvement towards operational excellence. The customer deferred their planned migration and continued on a support contract because they saw value in what we were doing.

Noel Sebastion
CS&S Manager Greater China

LEAN PICKINGS

► Polling customers for their feedback is critical; both general surveys and transaction-based surveys can be used for this purpose.

► Measurements need to be standardized across the organization, both in terms of what is measured and how it is measured.

► It is critical to complement internal measurements with external measurements reflecting the customer's perspective.

14

BOULDER SHIFTING
Smart Changes and Their Results
Sunit Prakash

*In which empowered staff members run kaizens
across the globe, with results clear for all to see.*

ARDIN VLOT KICKED OFF THE WHOLE Up To Excellence effort
by bringing the middle management team together. During
the first transformation event, using a key exercise he ran in a
safe and supportive manner, he polled the team and identified
which 'boulders' or issues prevented us from improving our
customer satisfaction.

I have no doubt Vlot and the SLT were already very aware of
some of these issues, but perhaps some comments identified
new concerns. Others helped to validate suspicions the SLT
already had.

We created and sorted an inventory of all the boulders, and
identified easy-to-shift ones. Then came Lean training – first
for the middle managers, then for each of the support centres.
Targets were assigned. Communication was fast, frequent,
personal and urgent. Phone reviews with Vlot were held, and
he later visited each support centre. And kaizens sprang up
everywhere.

One frequent complaint we received from customers (which became known as 'The Black Hole of Calcutta') was that they would often report cases, but then would never hear back from support centres about them. It was as if, once they were reported, they disappeared into a black hole. There would be no solutions or updates from our support centres.

Evidently customers felt their problems were not being addressed. To overcome this, kaizen events developed a process to ensure that customers got regular updates on the status of their reported cases. It was not okay to be silent about the progress on the case until the case was resolved. Customers wanted to be informed about what the support analysts and product engineers were doing as they investigated their cases and resolved them.

Our other main complaint related to Promised Resolution Date. When reported cases were confirmed as a newly found defect, a bug-fix would then be developed. But often the product engineers developing these bug-fixes frustrated customers by not informing them when the bug-fix was going to be ready.

The Promised Resolution Date kaizen recognized that product engineers were often reluctant to name a date because they didn't feel comfortable to commit to timeframes stating when the solutions would be available. "Why promise when I can't be sure when I can fix the problem?" was the prevailing attitude. This needed a mindset change. In addition, the kaizen identified a need for an additional field to be added into the Case Management System. Now customers could have access to the status information, and a likely date when the bug-fix would be ready.

While initially a number of kaizens were run at a global level, kaizens began to spring up locally as Lean trickled down to reach each support analyst in each support team. Sydney ran a kaizen on how to reduce the end-to-end resolution time of cases held in Sydney. This identified orphan cases that were left hanging with no owners, the cherry-picking of easy cases, and the problem of some analysts sitting on a large number of cases they assigned to themselves.

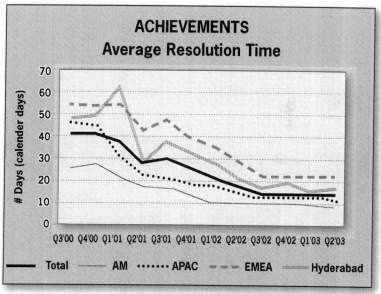

Graph showing decrease in average resolution time globally and across all regions

Sydney started to run daily stand-up meetings and used reports to show trends and identify discrepancies. And we began to see this ownership and empowerment everywhere. The result was that backlog started declining, quality of solutions started improving, and customer satisfaction started to increase!

Another kaizen event in Mumbai established that a major portion of their cases arose from India localizations made to the software. These localizations were maintained by a partner in India, and it was this partner who developed bug-fixes for the localizations whenever defects were reported. While the team knew that this arrangement was giving them pain, they didn't know how much!

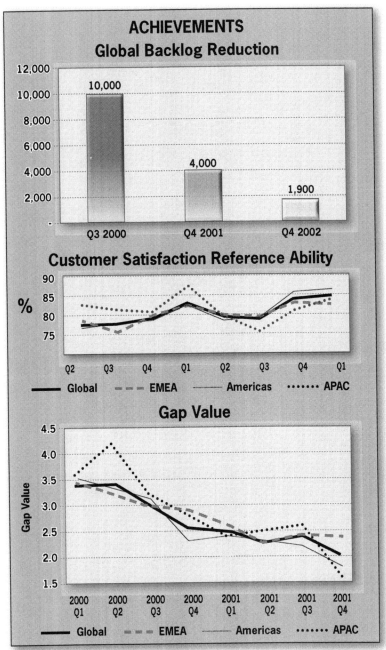

Graphs showing reduction in backlog, increasing customer satisfaction referenceability, and decrease in the customer dissatisfaction gap value

A quick study showed that for just a single defect, an average eighteen separate communications via email or fax occurred before the customer problem was resolved. The team recommended that software maintenance of the localizations be brought in-house. Additional staff were hired, and within three months of making the changes things began to get better.

Some kaizen improvements were fairly simple and were made within a couple of hours. These were the Just Do It improvements. One example was that some of the support centres in APJ didn't have adequate modem dial-out facilities. A decision was quickly made to acquire additional facilities or upgrade existing ones.

At the other end of the spectrum were the major, complex improvements. An example was the 7x24 Follow the Sun project to raise service levels and operational capability – also an opportunity to sell more 7x24 support to our customers.

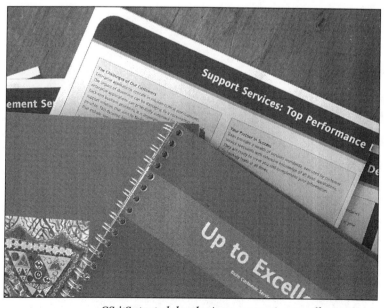

CS&S started developing new services to offer its clients

A further example of a complex project was the development of the patch installation tool. Until this tool was made available, customers would sometimes install new patches without properly considering either the patches they had already installed previously, or the program customizations they had performed on the system. Sometimes these new patches would conflict with patches already installed on the customer system, and in some instances they would override them, which meant that previously fixed defects would reappear! In other instances they would override the customizations that had been made previously, causing the system to behave incorrectly. The patch installation tool resolved these problems by checking for prerequisite patches and also installing the patches in the correct directories or folders.

In between simple and complex projects were the mid-sized ones. These were the typical kaizen projects which were worked on during a four- or five-day kaizen event, with the aim of completing the project within thirty days.

The kaizen improvements that took place across the organization shifted the boulders that were blocking enhanced performance. The result was a transformation which came from executing the Up To Excellence strategy, driven by the management and strongly supported by the 'masses'. Lean thinking was now widely accepted and had become the norm in terms of how to do things. Lean vocabulary became commonplace as employees and managers alike continued to look for ways to improve.

The two-year transformation beginning in the third quarter of 2000 brought outstanding improvements. The Overall Customer Satisfaction Gap Score fell from 3.4 to 1.4 – better than the target of 2.0. With this improvement, Customer Reference Ability shot up from 60% when we started to reach 85% globally. We had started Operation Breeze with a huge case backlog of 10,000. By the end of two years we had cut this drastically by almost 80%. As a consequence of this our Resolution Time also fell to a quarter of what it had been before.

Service quality was also important for us. The quality of our solutions was measured by First Time Right Rate (FTRR) percentages. Globally the FTRR increased from 94% to reach 96% over this period, and in some regions reached as high as 99%.

To say that the customers were happy with the new situation would be a clear understatement. All this had taken place because we had a powerful but pragmatic strategy, and middle managers and employees had caught the vision. We were able to engage them effectively by leveraging the Lean platform.

As our processes improved, support analysts repeatedly discovered opportunities in the customer base arising from particular customers' deficiencies. These deficiencies sometimes arose from a lack of skills or training of customer personnel, or from a shortage of personnel, or sometimes simply because opportunities to improve management of the system or optimize it were left untouched. This eventually led CS&S to develop new services it could offer. The ITIL framework was

Agility, Flexibility and Success

I had never envisaged that Operation Breeze, Lean practice and kaizens at CS&S would have such a long-lasting impact on my career. Reducing our backlog to 40% in 9 months, or taking over localization support from our localization partner . . . sometimes I was a foot soldier on the front, and sometimes first line manager.

These projects have made me a true and successful support professional. For sure, Ardin Vlot was ahead of his time and CS&S was the best team I have ever worked with.

Rajeev Dixit
Support Team Leader, Mumbai

used to build service blueprints for the development and sale of these services.

Alongside the use of ITIL, CS&S aspired to become ISO certified. Lean directly supports the implementation of ISO quality management systems. The next chapter highlights how ITIL was leveraged for the development and subsequent launch of new services, and also touches on how Lean supports ISO quality management system implementation.

LEAN PICKINGS

▶ The leader needs to identify and prioritize the issues.

▶ A good leader will validate his views with feedback directly from the field, whether front line support analysts, or the direct voice of the customer.

▶ Training and empowerment is a must for successful organizational change.

▶ Without strong leadership sponsoring and support, improvement projects will not succeed.

▶ With improved processes come better quality, improved staff engagement and new business opportunities.

15

NEW OPPORTUNITIES
Additional Revenues, ITIL and ISO
Sunit Prakash

In which Lean practices open doors to new business opportunities and quality certification.

SUPPORT ANALYSTS IN SYDNEY OBSERVED A spike in cases whenever a new service pack was released. Customers would try to load these, run into trouble, and start logging calls for assistance. Not wanting to work in a never-ending case factory, the Sydney analysts decided to load service packs on an internal server before releasing them to customers. The idea was: "Let's get to the root cause and fix it, so that the customer never has to call us!"

By loading the service packs they were able to uncover the pitfalls and put out additional guidance notes for customers. They could also feed back development improvements for the next service pack.

The support analysts quickly discovered customers were happy to pay for this service. It could be delivered remotely, no travel was required, and incidents and cases could still be handled as the job was running on the customer system. The revenues were not large, so the consulting organization allowed the support centre to handle this business – and the price offered very good value to customers. This was a win-win situation all around! It also meant fewer calls to the support centre, a proactive service to the customer, and more interesting and meaningful work for the support analysts!

This did not go unnoticed by Ardin Vlot and his management team. The consulting organization was engaged in major projects doing implementation work, and was generally stretched for resources. This kind of lower revenue, highly technical consulting was not of interest to them. An opportunity existed between the work they did and the work that Support did. There were dollars being left on the table.

In countries like Japan, where the consulting organizations were already highly stretched performing new implementations, a business opportunity would present itself the moment someone spoke to a customer in the installed base. And so APJ started work on offering remote monitoring and performance tuning of the application from our Global Support Centre in Hyderabad. Our portfolio initially comprised new Education and Knowledge Management Services, Application Management Services, Performance Tuning and Health Checks, but there was always a demand for assistance with loading new service packs, and performing migrations to new versions and upgrades.

To watch traditionally back-office support team leaders and managers turn their hand to business development was fascinating. It was amazing enough to see mild-mannered support analysts sell services in a location like Sydney, but to see the same behaviour from normally very shy Hyderabad-based teams was totally mind-blowing!

Soon our scorecards also started to include the dollars and activity related to this type of work. This came as a direct result of using Lean to improve processes, reducing case backlogs but not reducing staff. Staff freed up from reduced escalations now began deploying themselves to bring in additional revenues by performing activities that were of value to the customer and that also reduced pain to themselves.

A bit about ITIL and how it was used

Heymen Jansen utilized the ITIL v2 framework to put together service blueprints to show customers their pain points, and how CS&S could assist and position new services for them. (ITIL – IT Infrastructure Library – was then emerging as a global best-practice framework for providing IT services to business.) All middle managers received training to the Foundation Level of ITIL, and additional business development workshops were run.

	Backlog	Backlog Age	Resolution Time	First Time Right Rate	CCFF	Cust Sat Gap from Prognostics	Revenues from Standard Support	Additional Revenues	Initiatives & Notes
APJ SCORECARD									
Targets									
Week 14	met	met	met	met	met	met	on budget	nil	ITIL v2 Foundation in Hyderabad
Week 15	met	met	met	met	not met	exceeded	on budget	on target	Education deal closed in Singapore
Week 16	exceeded	met	met	met	not met	exceeded	on budget	on target	Kaizen in Mumbai, Tokyo & Sydney
Week 17	not met	met	met	met	exceeded	exceeded	on budget	on target	Softskills training, pilot 7x24 follow the sun support

The APJ scorecard showing operational metrics, additional revenues and the status of quarterly objectives

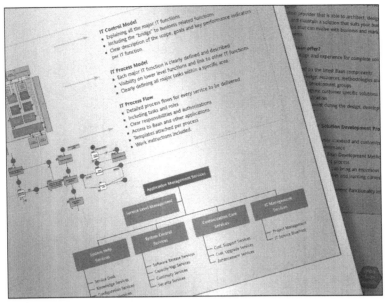

Sample A2 service blueprints

Growing the Support Business

As we made our way on the Lean Transformation journey, we focused on reducing waste, implemented Lean principles, empowered our people, and undertook other initiatives to grow our business.

For traditional software companies, the usual business model is very simple: sell software, sell implementation services and sell support. We wanted to change that because we felt that this traditional approach was insufficient for a long-term customer relationship and commitment. So we began to build a business model to create long-term service contracts with customers. And of course the model had to be lean! So we introduced a new service within the company, Application Management Services, to support long-term relationships, resulting in a recurring revenue model with higher value-adding services.

After a few months a small team of three people developed a market strategy, set up virtual champion teams around the world, and began to

The service blueprints were highly effective. Rolled up A2 sheets of process maps in the style of architectural blueprints were opened on a client's boardroom table, and used to walk the client through ITIL processes to identify points at which Baan CS&S could assist in relieving their pain. Typically these were in the areas of change, release, configuration and knowledge management.

While Baan CS&S did not use the ITIL framework for its own operations it was ahead of the curve, already using for its own service improvement many elements which were to be included in ITIL v3.

ITIL v3 has the following components: *Service Strategy, Service Design, Service Transition, Service Operations,* and *Continual Service Improvement.* Let me briefly summarize how these elements played out in Baan CS&S.

train local account managers and consultants, and . . . closed our first contracts. Our strategy was: think big, start small, act fast!

It was fascinating to see how a small team could make this happen in such a short time, beginning from scratch. I believe that this was possible only because we were supported by many, many colleagues who were a part of our Lean Transformation journey. Even with our small successes, everybody celebrated with us. I had never experienced such strong team spirit before embarking on Lean, and I have never experienced anything similar again in my career. Now years later and having left the company, I still receive news from former colleagues that the Application Management Services continues to be an important part of the overall business model of the company.

Without our Lean Transformation journey we could never have achieved this. I'm still very pleased and honoured that I was a part of this fantastic team!

Heymen Jansen
Director Application Management Services

Service Strategy includes the definition of Business Service Requirements, determination of market space, IT policies and strategies, a service portfolio, demand management and financial management. Vlot understood the business requirements and drivers of his own organization and those of his customers – and developed a service strategy to address them. "Service improvement to improve customer satisfaction and protect and grow revenues with the same or fewer resources" was the mantra.

As required by *Service Design,* Service Levels of Support were set and formalized and promised to the customers. A service catalogue listing a portfolio of new services and offerings was constructed by the business development team in the Netherlands.

For *Service Transition,* the Release and Deployment Management was transformed, and Transition Planning and Support and the Change Management process were improved. Service Validation and Testing was also improved to address the issues that arose in the Service Operation space (read: Support Centres and Customers) downstream.

In *Service Operation* itself there was a huge focus on Knowledge Management, and Problem Management was formalized. Of course Incident Management, Access Management and the Request Fulfilment processes were improved (ITIL's Event Management process being less relevant to our business).

Continual Service Improvement was central to our strategy. The improvements in Service Transition and Service Operation were underpinned by a desire to improve Customer Satisfaction, and driven by the People (capital P on purpose). Lean was the method Baan CS&S used to drive Continual Service Improvement.

As it turns out, many of the practices we developed were independently distilled and made available in ITIL. But there are other IT Service Management frameworks for those in the know, including Tipu by Rob England, the Universal Service Management Book Of Knowledge (USMBOK) by Ian Clayton, Microsoft's Microsoft Operations Framework 4.0, TM Forum's eTOM (enhanced Telecom Operations Map), and of course ISACA's CoBIT and the ISO 20000 standard. In addition there are resources available from the Help Desk Institute, The Service Desk Institute, and notably from Françoise Tourniaire of FTWorks.

Baan CS&S did not start off with a "Let's use ITIL to solve our problems" approach. It was a "What is the problem, what is to be achieved, what is stopping us from getting there, how do we get there and how do we know when we have arrived? – and let's use Lean to get there" approach.

The net nett is that Baan CS&S did not 'do ITIL'. Its ITIL engagement was driven by its desire to deliver value to the customer. Intuitively and instinctively it did what it had to do to improve its internal processes. These were processes that any IT organisation performs to deliver services to their customers – and so by definition they were ITIL processes.

Our metrics were now global and consistent, thanks to the SIS. We had a global case management system which underpinned not only our planning and reporting, but also our processes. All of our support analysts knew what we were about and what we wanted to achieve. We had numbers to show us if we were on the right track.

More importantly, to support our overall vision we had also enunciated our Quality Objectives – in fact, to be Best In Class was itself a Quality Objective. In words, deeds and actions, the CS&S team was demonstrating a commitment to quality.

ISO Certification

We now had the core elements in place for ISO 2000 certification. We had the right vision, we were doing the right things, and we were doing them for the right reasons. We had total alignment from top to bottom, and we could measure and demonstrate our performance. What we did not have was a Quality Management System Process Model.

So we took what we had:

- Business Planning and Reporting – business plans, customer satisfaction reporting, target setting, performance forecasts, workload forecast
- Resolving Customer Issues – customer case handling, defects, customer feedback, escalations, intensive care, critical incident support, multi-vendor support, maintenance policies
- Enabling Activities – alliance management, business management, supply management, support innovations, marketing and communications, human resource management, human capital development, enhanced support services

The Power and Simplicity of Lean

Initially I viewed Lean as just another management initiative to tick the box for. But after the initial introduction and spending more time understanding what was required, I saw such great value that it transformed me personally and also transformed the team that I managed.

Simple day-to-day activities we managed to streamline and improve made little

. . . and overlaid them with the Quality and Management activities.

These included creating and maintaining a Quality Manual, documenting the processes (including a process to keep the manual up to date), performing quality audits, and taking corrective and preventive actions.

Standard process documents outlining our drivers, our operating framework and our key processes were created and put in place in a central repository. The drivers and operating framework came from Vlot and the SLT team at a strategic level. The procedures manual was at an operational level.

With ISO 9001:2000 certification come regular audits. This is how our Sydney audit went. The auditor from KEMA turned up and first talked to Bansal, who was our local Support Manager at the time.

Question: what does your team do?

Answer: we provide technical product support to our customers.

Question: how do you manage this?

steps in making the overall team a lot easier to manage. I recall that we visually presented our team targets by putting them up on one of the columns in the office, allowing the team to see the improvements we were making on a regular basis. Another visual method we used was to send daily emails to each of the team members giving them updates on their achievements from the day before.

The Lean drive improved the overall work and team environment for me. I continue using the simple Lean principles both in my personal and professional life.

Osama Kort
CS&S Manager, Australia & New Zealand

Answer: we have standard procedures, we perform daily checks and reports.

Question: where is your procedures manual?

Answer: online so that we have one version and everyone can use it (shows it to him).

Question: where are your daily reports?

Answer: in the printer tray, it runs overnight (shows him today's report, and yesterday's, and the day before and the day before that. . . .)

Question: what are your key measures?

Answer: Customer Satisfaction, Backlog, Backlog Age, First Time Right Rate (takes him to the 'wall of frames' where customer letters of appreciation and positive accolades have been framed and displayed).

The auditor had never seen an organization as organized as this. His comment to us was "The Support organization far exceeded the requirements of ISO 9001:2000"!

The ISO/IEC 20000 has since been released and it aligns closely with the ITIL v3 framework. I have no doubt had Baan CS&S gone in for ISO/IEC 20000 certification it would have had no problems in achieving it, because it demonstrated in "thoughts, deeds, actions and results – the successful adoption of an integrated process approach to deliver effectively managed services to meet business and customer requirements".

In the next chapter we turn our attention to the transformation events and other staff gatherings. This chapter provides more insight into what went on.

LEAN PICKINGS

► Start with the BIG issues and questions – what is the problem and what are you trying to achieve?

► Use existing industry frameworks to provide guidance and structure to your transformation program.

► Find a methodology to drive the change for improvement.

► Measure, improve, measure.

► ITIL v3 is a framework for organisations to manage and provide IT services; but there are others.

► Continual Service Improvement is a key element of the ITIL framework.

► Lean lends itself to Continual Service Improvement.

► ISO/IEC 20000 is the standard for IT Service Management.

► Further guidance can be obtained from the new version of CoBIT (v5) which incorporates elements of 'value' ValIT and RiskIT.

16

ALL ABOARD
Leadership, Communication, and Organizational Transformation
Robert Oh

In which a leader mines his own life experiences to communicate vision, and events are held to inspire, involve and leverage the talents of every employee.

INITIALLY TRANSFORMATION EVENTS WERE USED TO create a powerful coalition for change. Subsequent events sought both to sustain this organization-wide drive for improvement, and also to steer the organization toward its new direction of proactive field services to help clients and reduce the number of calls coming in, while also harvesting new revenue opportunities.

These events were also a platform to communicate how we were progressing and to encourage the middle managers to keep going. Both the transformation events and other, more local staff gatherings, were opportunities to inspire, teach, reinforce, hearten and deepen our sense of shared identity and purpose.

During our first transformation event Ardin Vlot asked me to speak about Operation Breeze. I recall that I wanted to explain how Operation Breeze would help our company in strategic terms, because I felt some managers and employees might incorrectly see it as simply another operational initiative to cut the backlog, like so many we had previously tried without success. It was much more than that, and I wanted to make this point clear.

TOTAL STRENGTH
Black to White is 2:1

Illustration of Force to Space Ratio

To introduce this topic I began with a military concept known as Force to Space Ratio. In simple terms, Force to Space Ratio refers to the concentration of forces you have in a given geographical area or space. The more you concentrate your forces, the higher your Force to Space Ratio becomes.

I then presented how the math behind this concept worked, showing how a smaller force could overcome a much larger, more diffuse one by concentrating its forces and winning localized battles. Step by step the larger force is overcome in piecemeal fashion in localized battles where the smaller force has a higher Force to Space Ratio. This concept links to the idea of a niche strategy.

Smaller companies that cannot compete with the 'big boys' tend to adopt a niche strategy, concentrating their limited resources to compete in one or two target markets. This allows them to better meet the needs of their target market and gives them an edge over the competition.

We had to be equally focused with Operation Breeze if we wanted to be successful in reducing the backlog. It was like chopping down a tree: our axehead had to be razor sharp to cut till only the stump was left. To succeed with Operation Breeze *we* needed to be razor sharp – and success would give our company an edge over competitors.

In speaking with and engaging with employees wherever I went, I would often make use of military analogies. All male Singaporean citizens do a compulsory stint of National Service, and this was where I received my military training. As a platoon leader during my two and a half years of National Service I had my first taste of leadership, and I always enjoyed leading my men through the rigorous training exercises.

I saw my role in leading Operation Breeze no differently. I had to lead, I had to encourage and I had to motivate. The end objective had to be made clear and it had to be uppermost in the minds of everyone involved. We were a team with a mission.

During our second transformation event I spoke about all the different elements of Operation Breeze, again relating them to military concepts. These ranged from the morale and motivation so needed for a

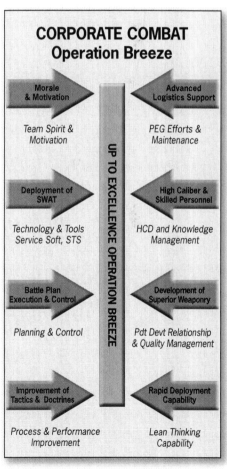

Illustration of the different elements of Operation Breeze

battle, to the need for proper execution of a battle plan with a control dashboard (our equivalent to constant intelligence information that needs to come from the field), and the requirement for a solid logistics supply line, which to us was the role of PEG.

One of Lean's key concepts was the idea of empowerment and self-directed teams. It was new to the organization, and not everyone understood what it meant. To illustrate the idea of empowerment and self-directed teams I would often tell of an experience I had during my National Service (NS).

Our unit had gone for an overseas training stint. On the first day of training there I was acting as exercise controller for a section-level tactical topography exercise. The terrain was quite tough: undulating hills and mountains. The weather was very hot, but as we largely travelled through forest we had the benefit of shade for the most part. We were on a mountain in the middle of nowhere several hours into the exercise when without any warning the section leader collapsed, unconscious. He had suffered a heat stroke.

In my experience NS men don't generally take their training very seriously. They don't seem all that interested to learn, like workers in a company who aren't really interested in doing their best. When that happens, there is much waste.

Yet when their section leader collapsed I watched these men move amazingly quickly to get branches and put together a makeshift stretcher with a ground sheet. Heat stroke can be fatal, and they knew this. There was urgency in their actions. They needed no instructions about how to put together the stretcher – they knew exactly what to do. My part was to do the map reading and get us to the safety evacuation point in the shortest possible time while they all worked together without any coercion to double him out of there, up and down the hills for hours, till we reached the evacuation point.

They knew what to do 'when the rubber hit the road'. All I needed to do was to point them in the right direction, and they ran – like a self-directed team empowered to do what they had to do.

I would tell this story to illustrate the idea of empowerment and self-directed teams. There is so much talent in any organization, as in the case of these NS men. The challenge is finding out how to engage with them in such a way that they will give their best. This is what we had to learn during our Lean journey so that the full talent of our organization could be put to good use and driven to its goals.

Soon after the success of the first transformation event, a decision was taken to hold such meetings every six months. The first meeting was the commencement of our journey – to rally the troops, have them catch the vision, build commitment, inform them of their goals, and begin the Lean journey with tangible and visible efforts. Teams of middle managers were created to tackle the top eight issues the organization was facing. Work began during the meeting itself, and in the following months these teams presented the fruit of their efforts and successes to Vlot and the rest of the SLT.

Our second transformation event focused on the gains we had made in cutting back the case backlog, the result of substantial improvement efforts made by the organization all around the world. It looked at where we were and where we should go next, with the necessity to keep up momentum with the launch of Breeze II.

The theme of this second meeting was *Lean Transformation*. It included several exciting sessions exploring creative problem solving and teamwork, something we wanted to promote and strengthen. In one of these sessions two teams had to create mosaic artwork beginning with a specific concept. But there was a catch. Each team not only had limited material and

One of the mosaic artworks created

colours to work with to complete their art piece, but also had to break their base material into small pieces before they were allowed to use it. It was an exercise which required planning towards a clear and predefined goal, and team co-ordination and co-operation as team members worked together to create their art piece. Everyone in the team had to be creative but yet work as part of a team within the time and material constraints they faced.

Another team was given the task to write, rehearse and sing a Lean Transformation song. For the next two hours the team

Lean: Making Everyone Entrepreneurial

Our team's name was "Oriental Massage", which made people laugh. Many attendees felt tired during our long work sessions. So we thought many of them would want some refreshment, including finger pressure massage.

Santosh was the leader of our team. Ronald Bussink was also a member and there was another lady from Israel, though she had to return earlier.

Santosh worked on the marketing and sales. He gathered many people, and to demonstrate our services we did the first three or four people for free.

got down to work and eventually came up with a three-part song with words reflecting this theme. "Lean is the way, we have to make it better," went the words. "Don't worry be happy, we can do it together/ Join in, sing with us . . ." The performance brought the house down.

Another of the mosaic artworks

By the time of our third transformation event, so much productivity improvement had been realized that CS&S was easily able to redeploy more than 10% of its resources. By this stage the game plan had changed. The CS&S resources were experienced and valuable, and we now wanted to deploy them

We had so many customers – some ladies asked for it twice. I also massaged Ardin during dinner time.

Anyway, I was really exhausted from this work, physically. After I used up all the wet tissues (pre-moistened wipe) for cleaning my hands, I had to rush to a restroom to wash my hands each time. Nobody wanted to be touched with hands used to massage others!

I think our team came in second place for either Revenue or Profit. But I am sure we were tops for Customer Satisfaction in spite of our high price strategy. Three minutes for three euro – expensive! But Santosh helped by convincing the customers. And Ronald recorded the sales in the system. No one wanted him to do massage, so he changed his role and did something else.

Shinya Takahashi
CS&S Manager Japan

for innovative new services which would offer our customers additional value.

This third event focused on making everyone an entrepreneur and businessman. A business game was played throughout that meeting during the breaks, lunches and before dinner time, and teams had to think creatively to develop and sell services that would earn them the most profit.

One of the teams in this business game sold Oriental Massage Services. They were a big hit and made lots of profit. I was playing the role of an AMR Market Analyst, and my job was to go around and interview the teams to collect information that was newsworthy. When I came to this team I couldn't help noticing that only one person was providing the massage services.

I asked the team leader incredulously how many workers he had in his team – only one, he promptly told me. "What are the other four team members doing?" I asked. He said, "Well we have one CEO – myself – one Marketing Manager, one Sales Manager, and we also have one Admin Manager." I was intrigued. In spite of having so many managers and only one worker they still managed to come a close second in the game by having a lot of sales.

A Strong Transforming Breeze

Year 2001, location Mumbai, department Customer Support. A team of young dynamic go getters, striving hard to constantly achieve service levels at customer expectations, fighting the battle with insufficient tools and a product which was mission critical, but extremely complex.

Then came a strong Breeze – a new tool to be used as the main weapon for improving service levels for the customer. Stand-up meetings, empowered teams, self commitments, escalation teams, review meetings, Critical Customer listings – all formed a part of this toolkit which helped

Teams working on issues during one of the transformation events

So as part of the game, I reported that evening on this team which had done well, made a lot of money and almost taken first place. Yet its five-person team contained four managers and only one worker! (I left out the fact that the one worker, the Japan Support Manager, was the only one who knew how to give a proper massage.) It caused a lot of amusement.

At another occasion we were having a staff event at Hyderabad. Teams were formed, this time not to work on improve-

this team bring down a backlog of customer issues by 50% in a timeframe of four months.

The Mumbai team adopted the Lean transformation process for its most critical and difficult process of handling customer issues for a product which was localised heavily for Indian laws. Lean transformation helped reduce duplication, reduced turnaround time and eliminated waste. End result: a cost saving of approximate USD 250k!

Ravi Kabbur
Director Baan Global Support India

ments, but to come up with singing and skit items for the staff event. I remember doing the number *Twist and Shout* with several of the guys. We all had a wonderful time.

Celebrations and fun were an important part of our journey. Both the global transformation events and other more localized gatherings were times of learning, camaraderie and inspiration in a light-hearted atmosphere.

In leading and speaking at these events, one of my roles was to build awareness of how APJ was different from the other regions. It was clear that we were the most complex region because of language issues, the need for translations, special multi-byte requirements in the software, and the localizations needed in the software product. In particular I had to emphasize the culturally unique high service expectations of our Japanese customers so that I would get the cooperation and help of units from other regions if a need ever arose.

I took every opportunity to do this wherever I addressed employees. As a market, Japan clearly has the highest service expectations in the world. The ethos of Japanese suppliers is to move heaven and earth to help their customers should they ever experience problems with their products or services. This is the reason why, in almost every multinational company I have come across, the Japan office would demand its own local support capability. It couldn't depend on overseas offices with little understanding of the culture and psyche of a typical Japanese customer to support its market.

If you have a good and reliable product and your service level to your customers is high, the Japanese will pay you top dollar for your product and you will be very successful there. On the other hand, if you have a bad product and your service is poor, you're dead – you will never be successful in Japan.

While these assertions conveyed important truths, personal stories made the strongest impact on audiences. I would often illustrate my assertions with stories of my own experiences in Japan.

At one time I had travelled to Japan for a week. Just before lunch on the last day, I returned from the office to my room to pack up. For some reason I felt I should check whether all my travel claim documents were in order. I discovered that the bus ticket I had purchased on the day I arrived to travel from Narita Airport to the hotel was missing. I searched but couldn't find it. It was only a bus ticket, but a bus ticket for a ride from the airport to the hotel in Japan can be quite expensive!

I took a look in the waste bin in case I had accidentally thrown it away. No, it was not there. Remembering that I had thrown some stuff away into the waste bin that morning, I thought to myself that the bin must have been emptied by the housekeeping ladies I had just seen outside my room.

So I opened my door and asked them. I showed them my empty bin. The two ladies didn't understand my English, and began to speak to each other quite animatedly. Since they couldn't understand me, I thought to myself I wouldn't pursue this and said "It's okay, never mind." They left and I resumed packing.

In less than five minutes there was a soft knock on the door from a hotel supervisor. He enquired if he could help me and I told him about the ticket, but I added that it was alright, meaning never mind and don't worry about it any more. He then left.

After another five minutes there came another knock. There he was again, this time holding up a piece of paper. He asked whether it was the ticket I was looking for. I told him no, and added that my ticket was orange in colour. Then I tried again to tell him that it was alright – they didn't have to keep looking for the ticket.

He left, and as soon as I closed the room door I had a strange feeling: "Oh no, I hope they're not still looking for it!" I opened my door to take a peek. The supervisor was giving instructions to three housekeeping ladies. They started to wheel their cart to the end of the corridor. They went through the large doors with me following just behind them. They continued chatting among themselves, and began to spread out some thin plastic sheets on the ground.

I was beginning to feel quite embarrassed about the stir I had caused and tried to tell them once again not to bother any more – that they should stop searching for the ticket. But before you knew it, two of them had already overturned the garbage bags from their carts onto the plastic sheets and were literally on their knees searching for this silly old bus ticket!

Because of language reasons I couldn't really communicate with them. So I gave up trying to tell them to stop and went back to my room. Two minutes later there was another knock on the door, and there was the supervisor again, this time holding up my orange bus ticket!

This is what I mean by the highest service levels being in Japan! I told this story wherever I went to emphasize my point that we had to make extra special effort when dealing with Japanese customers if we wanted to move ahead in the Japan market. The regular 'run of the mill' service would not be good enough.

As we journeyed on, clear signs of culture transformation towards service excellence did emerge. Teamwork and co-operation aimed at top-level customer satisfaction became the norm. An openness to try new ideas to make things even better was now commonplace – a significant difference from where we had come from.

We wanted our customers to be happy, and we were not holding anything back. Our journey was tough and yet fun, difficult yet invigorating. There was always so much energy, and any success itself brought much encouragement. We turn our attention in the next chapter to some of the more memorable things that took place during this journey.

LEAN PICKINGS

► Keep reinforcing and encouraging your organization to drive for improvement all the time.

► Raise awareness of important issues by engaging with employees with the aim of building a coalition for change.

► Look for additional revenue opportunities once you achieve increased productivity and have resource savings.

17

REFLECTING ON OUR LEAN JOURNEY

Robert Oh

*In which a leader on this journey considers its
transforming impact – both corporate and personal –
on the travellers.*

WE BEGAN OUR LEAN JOURNEY IN the autumn of 2000. Up
to that time Lean had been used primarily in manufacturing
companies; no services company had deployed Lean on such a
large or global scale before. The journey we were undertaking
was a maiden voyage to seas unknown.

But this was not really uppermost in our minds. We were concerned with two things: cutting our backlog dramatically, and
exploiting Lean concepts and ideas to help us do that – ideas
and concepts about eliminating waste, teamwork, empowerment, a flatter organization, an unprecedented emphasis on
upskilling, doing things right first time, and so much more.

There was some inertia at the beginning. When a copy of the
book *Lean Transformation* was sent to all CS&S managers, not
everyone read it. But Ardin Vlot's remarkable leadership was
able to win the hearts and minds of his direct team, and pretty
well the entire middle management ranks. This created a critical mass.

The first transformation event was exciting, well thought through, and executed with a finesse I have never seen repeated by any other leader in my 30-year career. And that great start to the journey didn't weaken, because the follow-up was also great. Unlike so many 'rah rah' sessions I have attended, the momentum clearly continued after the initial euphoria of the meeting had subsided.

As our leader, Vlot was truly inspirational and visionary, clear in what he wanted and yet meticulous at the same time – an extraordinary combination. Nothing was overlooked. His directions were always well defined, he always knew what he wanted, and he detailed all the right things. To say this was helpful in accomplishing our mission is of course a gross understatement.

As the journey continued our number of customer escalations, what we termed 'fires', became fewer. There were fewer fires to fight, more time to think strategically, and time to think about how to improve things even further. This is what managers are paid to do: to think through issues and then to execute. Our improving situation produced a snowball effect. The more improvements we made, the more time and resources were saved, and hence the more energy could be redeployed to make further improvements.

Significant credit for our Lean journey must be given to Maria Koral, our Lean Sensei and Advisor from Invensys. She was crucial in bringing these new Lean ideas to us, challenging us, providing us with the appropriate guidance and advice – always teaching, always using Lean language, and facilitating many of our kaizen

Ardin Vlot and Maria Koral

events all around the world. Her style was refreshing, her approach sound, her experience considerable. Maria was always present at our transformation events and often also at our SLT meetings. She was, you could say, 'iconic', the one who exemplified Lean.

Lean had to be embraced by everyone

But Lean had to be embraced by all, and had to be led at *every* level. We needed to appropriate the knowledge and experience she had and execute the improvements throughout our operation.

Lean ideas and Lean language were quickly adopted after we launched out on our journey. During discussions it became quite usual to hear comments like "Let's try to make things leaner"; "Let's cut the waste"; "Can we do this in a leaner way?" Kaizens became a key vehicle for us to spread this mindset. They provided employees with time to come out of their 'day jobs', take a step back and look at what was not going right, and then consider how to make those things better and leaner.

Everywhere I went I spent time telling customers what we were doing, how we were progressing. I did the same when I visited sales operations in various countries. There was a lot to tell. But even as things got better, I was often reminded in discussions with both customers and sales operations that we were not out of the woods yet. People have long memories. While things had got better, they still wanted more improvements. And of course they were right: there is always room for more improvement!

The two Asia Pacific centres of Mumbai and Hyderabad were crucial locations in APJ. Mumbai, the first centre to start up, housed some of APJ's most experienced support analysts. The Hyderabad location contained our mega-Global Support Centre as well as the region's PEG centre. Mumbai, in particular, played a central role in backfilling headcount at some of the local support centres where there were shortages, and in up-skilling these centres. It was always a pleasure to visit these locations, and each time I did, I would hold 'town hall' meetings with the staff to encourage them.

At a town hall meeting in the early days of the journey I remember speaking about how essential it was for us to accept change, because CS&S was undergoing rapid transformation due to all the process changes being made. I told a story about how difficult it can be to accept change.

In the battles fought during the American Civil War and many of those before them, it was usual to fight in large, tight formations. Infantry soldiers on both sides fought bravely standing in line, often in full view of the enemy, and fired large volleys at each other. The soldiers were not to break ranks to take cover when shot at, as foolish as this prohibition may seem. The wisdom of that day said you could not regain control of the troops if you were to allow this. So they chose instead to have them stand in line in the open and shoot at each other, even though it was virtually suicide.

It took quite some time before infantry doctrine changed to allow troops to get behind cover when fired upon. This happened only because rifles and newer weapons like machine-guns became much more lethal. So the inevitable change to the outdated Roman infantry doctrine of fighting in tight formations finally came. My point to them was that it took a long time coming . . . but CS&S now had to transform quickly. We couldn't afford unnecessary resistance to change.

On another occasion I spoke about weapons for breakthrough – that Lean, together with Operation Breeze, would give us a breakthrough. I used the illustration of how, long ago, trebuchets were used to break down the walls of strongly fortified positions to capture them – something I had learned from my sons, whose favourite pastime at that stage was playing computer games.

Castle walls were often many feet thick to keep attackers at bay. If the attackers wanted a quick win, almost always the only option open to them was to break down the walls and get into the fortress to win the battle. Trebuchets, the forerunners of artillery guns, were used to do this to win battles. I showed them pictures of trebuchets. Operation Breeze was our trebuchet to break the backlog. I was encouraging them to keep at it, not to lose focus, and to continue making improvements and achieving our goals.

One area where we needed a breakthrough was in implementation of the One Domain One Location concept. The Global Support Centre at Hyderabad occupied one floor and the PEG occupied another floor of our building. The support analysts were closer to the customer and hence understood their issues better, but they didn't know the program codes. The PEG engineers knew the program codes but didn't always appreciate the customer's problems.

Our intention was to co-locate the personnel from both sides based on the modules they supported, placing support analysts and PEG engineers side by side – effectively mixing the two departments. This would strongly support knowledge sharing between them, make for easy communications, and further boost teamwork. The bottom line was that we wanted to resolve customer issues even more quickly than we were already doing.

It was difficult to implement this change. PEG had concerns that it would increase interruptions to their work, resulting in productivity losses, and that PEG engineers could end up more heavily preoccupied with support issues than they should. Discussions wore on.

In the end a compromise was struck between both parties. A few key PEG engineers would be relocated into the Global Support Centre, but only for a specified period of time to work with the support analysts, to solve urgent issues when these arose, and also to carry out knowledge transfer activities. Though we didn't manage to effect a permanent change, results showed there was still significant value in doing this. Stronger bonds and informal networks were built between support analysts and PEG engineers. Support analysts learned the program code and the module designs, while PEG engineers came to appreciate the urgency of customer issues in far greater measure.

When we began our journey the relationship between support centres and PEG was somewhat fragile, and differences existed. Support analysts – the ones who had to 'face' the customers and depended on PEG to debug and develop bug-fixes – felt that PEG took too long to resolve the issues. PEG engineers, on the other hand, felt support analysts didn't always do a thorough enough investigation of the issues, and quite

Taking Lean Everywhere

The most important lesson I learnt from Operation Breeze was the different way one should approach process improvement. Experiencing Operation Breeze has helped me instinctively identify process flaws, and certainly suggest doable changes.

The idea of 'Takt time' – which translates to 'the beat of a process flow' – was an important learning point for me. When analyzing a process, improvement opportunities surface immediately when something doesn't go the way it's supposed to. Operation Breeze exposed us to various root-

often would wrongly determine that the problem was a bug in the software when in fact it was an implementation issue, a user error, or a failure caused by a customer's modification of the code.

As things got better cooperation improved markedly, teamwork solidified, and informal networks between Support and PEG became the norm. Once during an evening karaoke session after one of our APJ CS&S meetings in Yokohama, Japan, as we were singing *Let It Be*, Sunit Prakash began to substitute 'PEG' in place of the song's title phrase. It went something like this:

> *When I find myself in times of trouble PEG comes to me*
> *Speaking words of wisdom . . . PEG*
> *And in my hour of darkness she is standing right in front of me*
> *Speaking words of wisdom . . . PEG*
> *PEG, PEG, PEG, PEG*
> *Speaking words of wisdom . . . PEG*

It was hilarious, but it was also a symbol of the deepening relationship between Support and PEG. We had a whale of a time with all the Support Managers and the APJ PEG Manager that

cause analysis tools and techniques to help resolve process issues by finding the root causes of these problems, allowing us to fix them.

This was a significant discovery for me and has helped me throughout my career. The tools and techniques are not industry specific – in fact wherever you work there are processes, and those processes will have many improvement opportunities. One has to simply listen to the beat of customer demand and observe problems with the flow!

Santosh Menon
Manager PEG Finance

Sunit improving on Let It Be

evening. Morale was high, we were going places, and we were going to make history.

The further we journeyed on, the more we progressed. After two years customer reference ability for Support jumped right up to 90% levels in APJ, and 85% globally. It was an unprecedented feat.

I was delighted of course. When we began we were determined to make improvements, but I never envisaged the journey to be quite so exciting and fulfilling. Each week brought new ideas and thoughts. Each month brought more breakthroughs for our service level.

By the beginning of 2003, some 27 months after Operation Breeze began, we had made much headway and our focus had shifted toward offering new services. I sent a congratulatory email to all the CS&S APJ employees:

Lean in a Nutshell

The acquisition of Baan by Invensys brought to us a wonderful gift, the Lean philosophy. Basically I would summarize Lean as follows: do any action which improves the business of your customer, forward the rest to the trash. Think about your customers and you will find the answer to your questions and doubts.

Embracing the Lean philosophy led to the emergence of Operation Breeze. Operation Breeze was undoubtedly one of the most ambitious projects we executed, and although it had different results in the various

It has been an eventful 2002. We now lead all the regions with our aggressive approach in providing all kinds of optimization and other onsite services to our customers. This allows us to have better and stronger relationships with our customers and of course help the local country organizations earn more revenues and be more profitable. No doubt this will strengthen even further as we move towards our vision of being that one-stop provider of services where we create strong partnerships with the majority of our customers by getting more involved with them and helping them leverage more fully all the Baan solutions that they have invested in.

We recognize and wish to acknowledge the help we have received from others like Development and PEG as well. That ever readiness to help . . . may it become even more contagious!!! I look forward to even brighter days, months and quarters ahead. Everyone has worked very hard. Well done everyone. I would also like to wish all of you and your families a very Pleasant, Wonderful, Happy and Prosperous New Year.

One other thing to add, tomorrow Ravi Kabbur turns nine years old in Baan (actually he's now quite an 'old' kid). I

geographical regions, it was quite successful. We felt great satisfaction when we saw CS&S Barcelona, along with the team in Paris, meet its Operation Breeze goals.

A year before the purchase of the Baan business of Invensys by SSA Global, during an annual convention, I was awarded a Baan Outstanding Achievement Award – a recognition of the efforts of the team at CS&S Barcelona and Paris.

Jordi Morillas
Manager CS&S SouthEMEA

would like to congratulate him, and thank him for his efforts in leading the teams in India (BGS Hyderabad and CS&S Mumbai), for his never-say-die attitude (one of his great strengths), his Gung-Ho-ness, and his ever-ready support in singing the song 'Let It Be' to the substitute words of 'PEG' (if you don't understand what I mean, try it out, it makes for a more interesting song than the original). I still recall when I first joined Baan (not that long ago!), and Ravi flew in from Mumbai to take on a customer in Malaysia almost single handedly and scored with flying colours. He has certainly earned his 'stripes'. A true veteran indeed with 'battle scars' to show for it . . . Congrats Ravi.

Yes, we had many talented and determined veterans in APJ and the other regions who deserve special mention for their extra effort, their bold steps, their exceptional commitment and their never-say-die attitude. We had that special esprit de corps. It was hard work, but we enjoyed ourselves so much as well.

Following the excellent results at the end of 2002, Vlot sent a personal congratulatory letter to all CS&S employees, reiterating the magnitude of our achievement and his view on the role empowerment had played in our success. We had exceeded our goal to achieve an overall Customer Satisfaction Gap score of 1.5! Below is part of his letter:

Last quarter, for the first time in Baan's history, we achieved an overall performance GAP of 1.4. . . . One of the most striking things I have experienced is what happens if you empower others to do what you are supposed to do. In a way you 'lose' control, but in return you get a highly committed and dedicated team . . .

I had the privilege of leading our Lean charge with Operation Breeze. It was quite an honour, particularly since in those days it was rare for someone from Asia to be given responsibility to lead a significant global project in a multinational company.

In this experience I saw how Lean played out across our organization. I witnessed how managers at every level led their employees. I watched in amazement as teams all around the world became self-directed, striving hard to achieve the goals of their teams, their support centres and the global targets.

Robert Oh: I had the privilege of leading our Lean charge with Operation Breeze

Many of us had heard of the concept of self-directed teams, but few if any had actually seen them in action. Now we weren't depending on a few good people in specialized SWAT-style teams, but instead we involved and depended on the masses. The challenges we faced and the advancements we made were owned by every employee. Every employee took pride in what they did and the results they delivered.

The culture change we achieved was striking, and consequently the profile and standing of the CS&S organization rose tremendously. Colleagues and employees from other departments took notice of the positive changes and good news that kept coming in. Our customers were simply thrilled by the clear progress we made month by month as the teams dug in and then advanced, repeating this cycle month after month, quarter after quarter.

When we began offering the new optimization services another transformation began to happen: these backroom employees turned into entrepreneurs. They engaged with customers, and actively sought opportunities to sell additional onsite services and deliver them. When I set targets for these new services, I saw my reporting managers at each local support centre in APJ turn into businessmen and entrepreneurs along with their teams.

While the journey was about transforming CS&S, I now realize that so many of us were dramatically impacted by the experience of this journey, irrespective of our role during the journey or where we have gone in our careers since that time. So the journey was not only about organizational but also *personal* transformation. For most of us it was and will be the most remarkable, unique experience in our careers.

We all walked away after this experience forever changed, with vastly new and different perspectives about how to drive change and how to manage people. How important it is to empower the people. How un-Lean so many of the processes all around us in our organizations can be. How there is waste everywhere, how easily it can be removed, and how to go about doing this.

I was so blessed by this experience. I am truly thankful for the efforts made by every colleague and every employee. I am proud that we collectively achieved what we did. I am delighted when I think back on all the fun we had doing it. I am gratified to have run alongside everyone from CS&S on this Lean journey. I am honoured to have served together with my esteemed colleagues, and recollect their determination and resolve to win.

LEAN PICKINGS

▶ Strong leadership and clear purpose is essential to drive organization change through the strategic deployment of Lean.

▶ Use a sensei (a Lean consultant) for an extended duration to help you sustain your Lean journey.

▶ Co-location can be used to improve communications, support knowledge sharing and increase bonding and teamwork.

▶ Always remember to celebrate and to have fun!

▶ Transform every backroom employee into a business person.

▶ Leverage the 'power of the masses'.

18

OVER TO YOU

Robert Oh

*In which the authors wish you success as you progress
on your own Lean journey.*

OUR LEAN JOURNEY TOOK PLACE WHILE Baan was still a part
of Invensys. Invensys suffered losses during the US recession
from 2002 and 2003 and sold Baan to SSA Global Technologies
in June 2003. With this acquisition the journey continued
on, but at a diminished pace, and eventually ceased several
quarters after the acquisition.

In the years since we embarked on Up To Excellence, our Lean
journey, we had accomplished so much more than we could
have dreamed when we first began. But it was not primarily
about Lean or launching a Lean initiative. Lean was the platform supporting the changes, but effecting the improvements
was about achieving excellence in our operations. It was about
fulfilling a vision that won the hearts and minds of employees from early on. It was about teamwork, not about heroes
– about tapping the talents of CS&S employees by engaging
them and having them run the race with us. We involved all
the employees at every level to run with us. And we all ran
well.

We lived and breathed the Up To Excellence strategy and Operation Breeze. We eradicated waste everywhere. Lean was never looked upon as something extra to do on the side, something that added unnecessary burden on employees by giving them more work to do. It became a lifestyle, part and parcel of how we did things.

Lean has to be done strategically for it to help any organization to succeed in a major way. Lean has to feature in every pillar of your strategy so that no un-Lean part of your operation or organization clashes with the rest. Every organization has gaps. These gaps or weaknesses have to be taken care of or closed, so that your organization becomes stronger and leaner. The work and effort to close these gaps must go on continuously . . . this is what continuous improvement is about, isn't it?

The tools and techniques of Lean are many. They include, for instance, mistake proofing, waste elimination, pulling work instead of pushing, batch size reduction, co-location, kaizen events and so on – and they are very powerful. They are not hard to grasp or deploy, but until you learn how to embrace Lean fully, drive it strategically, and use it to help you robustly inspire your employees to run the race towards your vision, you will not tap its full potential to create great organizations. We had a lot working for us. We had a powerful vision, a strong and gifted leader, a potent strategy, a committed team, vigorous middle managers, motivated employees, a talented sensei, a formidable change project to improve performance, and a highly effective platform for change: Lean. These things do not come by themselves. They have to be built; they have to be led.

Strategic Lean deployment is therefore not just about Lean tools, or cutting waste, or training up some Lean leaders in your company, or even about executing kaizens – not that these things are unimportant. Instead, to create an intense drive towards total organizational transformation and excellence, your strategy must wholly embrace Lean. Lean must show up in every part of it. This is the only way to drive Lean powerfully and strategically.

Sunit and I are very grateful to have had this period of our careers graced by this experience. It has so impacted us that we caught a vision to tell this remarkable story, and a desire to bring this experience to other organizations which may benefit from it in a substantial way. We both believe strongly that this approach and success can be contextualized and hence replicated in almost any other organization.

Always continue to improve. We need not be satisfied with second-rate performance or mediocre improvement. Win the hearts and minds of your people and have them run the race together with you. They are more talented than you believe, and they can indeed run faster than you imagine. We wish you an enjoyable race . . . and may you run fast!

LEAN PICKINGS

▶ Lean is not your initiative to drive towards operational excellence, it is simply the platform that supports it.

▶ Involve everyone, involve the masses! Inspire them, inspire them, inspire them. Always keep going, never stop!

GLOSSARY

AM refers to the Americas regions, incorporating North, Central and South America.

AMR Market Analyst refers to an independent research firm which was sold to Gartner Research in 2009.

Apropos refers to the computer telephony integration platform vendor Apropos Technology, Inc.

ASEAN refers to Association of South East Asian Nations which included Indonesia, Malaysia, Thailand, Philippines and Singapore in 2002, and has since been extended to include Brunei, Burma (Myanmar), Cambodia, Laos, and Vietnam.

APJ refers to the Asia Pacific and Japan region.

Baan refers to Baan Corporation, a vendor of enterprise resource planning software which was acquired by Invensys in June 2000. The Baan brand name is now owned by Infor Global Solutions.

Baan Development refers to the Research and Development arm of Baan which built the new software products.

Breeze was the name of the global project to cut the case backlog significantly, and stands for *Backlog Reduction – Evolution to Excellence – Zillion Enjoyment*.

CAT was introduced by CS&S Americas to survey its customers and stands for *Courtesy, Accuracy and Timeliness*.

CCFF was a transaction-based survey system used by Baan CS&S and stands for *Customer Case Feedback Form*.

CoBIT is a framework for IT Governance and Control; ISACA's CoBIT provides guidance for executive management to govern IT within an enterprise.

CRM refers to Customer Relationship Management software to manage sales and marketing data and customer relationship management transactions.

CS&S is the name of the division for support and maintenance for Baan and stands for *Customer Service and Support.*

EMEA refers to the region of Europe, Middle East and Africa.

ERP stands for *Enterprise Resource Planning.*

eTOM stands for *enhanced Telecom Operations Map.* It is an ITIL-aligned Business Process Framework providing a comprehensive view of the key business processes a service provider requires to run its business.

FTRR stands for *First Time Right Rate* and refers to the percentage of output that is complete and without errors the first time through.

Gap Score is a measure which reflects the difference between the level of importance or expectation customers have in terms of service levels and what they perceive they are receiving.

Gartner refers to Gartner, Inc, an information technology research and advisory firm headquartered in Stamford, Connecticut, United States.

Invensys is a global engineering and information technology company headquartered in London, United Kingdom. Invensys is a trademark of Invensys plc.

ISACA, previously known as the Information Systems Audit and Control Association, provides information and guidance in the field of auditing controls for computer systems.

ISO refers to the International Organization for Standardization and is an international standard-setting body composed of representatives from various national standards organizations. The organization promulgates worldwide proprietary industrial and commercial standards. It has its headquarters in Geneva, Switzerland.

ISO 20000 or **ISO/IEC 20000** is a standard that defines the requirements for a service provider to deliver managed (IT) services.

ISO 9000 describes fundamentals of quality management systems and is part of the ISO 9000 family.

ITIL refers to Information Technology Infrastructure Library and is an Information Technology management framework that provides practices for Information Technology Services Management, IT development and IT operations. ITIL is a registered trademark of the United Kingdom's Office of Government Commerce.

Kaizen is a Japanese word which means *good change*. A kaizen is a continuous-improvement team project. Kaizens are meant to be rapid projects, the intent of which is to complete the project typically within 30 days from the kaizen event.

KEMA is a global provider of high-quality services including business and technical consultancy and certification. KEMA's corporate headquarters are located in Arnhem, Netherlands.

Lean Transformation originated in the mid-1990s when MIT researchers, eager to discover why Japanese automakers were so successful compared to the American automakers, studied Toyota and other Japanese auto producers and coined the term 'Lean' to describe what they found. 'Lean' is not an acronym. The term came about because it conjures images of speed, flexibility, agility and streamlining. The second term 'transformation' aptly describes the major changes to organization culture, management style, systems, processes, people and skills that take place in an organization which embraces Lean fully.

MoF, or **Microsoft Operations Framework,** delivers practical guidance on everyday IT practices and activities to establish and implement reliable, cost-effective IT services.

People Soft Inc was a company that provided enterprise resource planning software, and was acquired by Oracle Corporation in 2005. The PeopleSoft name and product line are now marketed by Oracle.

PEG refers to Product Engineering Group, the maintenance arm of the CS&S organization which developed the bug-fixes for the Baan ERP software.

PSD refers to Promised Solution Date, the promised date of resolution provided to customers whose case is transferred to PEG for a bug-fix to be developed.

Oracle refers to Oracle Corporation, an American multinational computer technology corporation that specializes in developing and marketing enterprise software products and database management systems. They are headquartered in Redwood Shores, California, United States.

Prognostics refers to the Prognostics Methodology® which is a registered trademark used for Providing Market Research and Related Consulting Services and owned by Tns Prognostics, Inc.

Response Time is defined as the time from when the call is first placed by the customer to the time when a call-back is made to the customer by the support centre. This is also the time when actual work begins on the issue being reported by the customer.

RiskIT is a framework for the management of IT-related business risk from ISACA; it provides an end-to-end, comprehensive view of all risks related to the use of IT.

SAP refers to enterprise resource planning software company SAP AG.

SCM refers to Supply Chain Management software meant for supply chain-related transactions.

SIS refers to Support Information System, an internal Baan CS&S business intelligence system.

SLT refers to the senior leadership team of Baan CS&S.

SSA Global Technologies was an enterprise resource planning software vendor which was acquired by Infor Global Solutions in July 2006.

Transformation events refer to powerful events targeted at the middle management ranks to drive and support transformation.

USMBOK refers to the Universal Service Management Book Of Knowledge which codifies and defines service management as a system.

ValIT from ISACA is a governance framework for Business Technology Management.

Value is defined as what the customer is willing to pay for. Non-value-added activities which are not required are considered waste.

Y2K refers to Year 2000.

Made in the USA
Lexington, KY
14 March 2012